Don't Miss Out:

The Ambitious Student's Guide to Financial Aid

by

Robert and Anna Leider
19th Edition

Address editorial correspondence to:
Octameron Associates, Inc.
P.O. Box 2748
Alexandria, VA 22301
(703) 836-5480

Address bookstore inquiries regarding purchases and returns to:
Dearborn Trade
520 N. Dearborn Street
Chicago, IL 60610
Outside Illinois, 800/245-BOOK
In Illinois, 312/836-4400 x270

ISBN 0-945981-84-8
PRINTED IN THE UNITED STATES OF AMERICA

Table of Contents

Appendices

Part I
Useful Things to Know

Chapter 1

Paying for College in the 90s

IT TAKES SPECIAL KNOWLEDGE

A college education is expensive. For some families it can be the largest expenditure they will ever make—more costly than the purchase of an average home and with fewer years to make the payments.

Even though this may not be what you want to hear, don't throw up your hands and walk away from college. Financial help is available—plenty of it. But there is more to getting aid than matching up a list of addresses to a pile of stationary and a supply of stamps. It takes special knowledge. For instance:

Knowing Who Gets the Aid. The theory of student aid holds that assistance should go to those who need it the most. In practice, assistance is more likely to find its way to those who know how to apply, when to apply and where to apply. By understanding the application process—by taking charge, you have an advantage over those who enter the process in a passive mode. That advantage translates into a greater chance of receiving aid, larger awards, and more desirable awards in terms of their composition (in other words, awards that do not have to be repaid).

Knowing About The Buyer's Market. Students are a scarce commodity. Competition for them is intense. This competition creates opportunities—opportunities that you should maximize.

Knowing Basic Personal Finance Techniques. There are investments, gifts, low-interest loans, education bonds, and special lines of credit. When properly used, these techniques can help your cash flow and be harnessed to student aid and reinforce its availability. When improperly used, they will cancel your eligibility for aid. You want to achieve the former and prevent the latter.

Knowing How to Tell Good Advice From Bad Advice. Advice on paying for college is plentiful. But not all of it is good. Some is dated. Some is wrong. And some is tainted by the self-interest of those who offer it.

Special knowledge is what this guide is all about. **Don't Miss Out** will teach you and your family how to formulate your own financial aid strategy—one that will lead you to a good, affordable higher education.

LOOKING FOR COLLEGE MONEY IS A FAMILY AFFAIR

A high school student told a newspaper reporter, "To ignore what your parents have to spend today, you've either got to be very thoughtless or very wealthy."

Well, you're not thoughtless, and you're not wealthy. That's why you're reading this book. Our advice to you: Read it not once, but twice—quickly the first time, to get the gist of the whole process; then slowly, taking notes on the college money options that best fit your family's situation.

After that, pass the book on to your parents. Why? Because paying for college is a family affair. You can't say, "Let them worry about it." They shouldn't say, "It's your problem." Everyone must be involved. The process must be well understood and the search must be started early. If these conditions aren't met, two things can and will happen. At best, the family will end up paying more for college than it should, or can afford. At worst, you will make a frantic, unplanned, last-minute college choice that is not in your best interest.

4

THE BIG PICTURE

The good news is that in 1995/96 approximately $44.5 billion in student aid will be available. Another bit of good news is that even more money is out there to be had. Uncle Sam's biggest student aid effort, the Stafford Loan, is an entitlement program. That means everyone who is eligible for a loan can get a loan. But it takes an application. As the great Confucius would have said: Apply forget—no loan you get. Experts have guessed that several billions more could be tapped if the participation rate of eligibles jumped to 100%.

The good news is balanced, as always, with bad news. Student expenses (tuition, room, board, books, fees, and transportation) will total $113.5 billion. A second item of bad news is that student expenses, in the years to follow, will continue to take huge annual jumps while student aid will level off (except for loan money) or even decline.

Take a good look at **Pie Charts A and B**. Note that Uncle Sam, the Colleges, the States, and Employer-Paid plans are the main sources of student aid. Not private scholarships. Our advice: When you start looking for financial aid, head for the tables with the biggest plates. Don't crawl under the table looking for crumbs. Unfortunately, many student aid seekers don't follow this advice. They make the search for crumbs—that one percent of the Student Aid pie which represents private scholarships—their number one priority. NOT SMART!

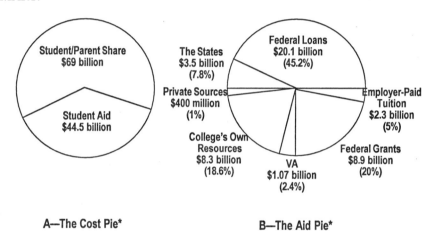

A—The Cost Pie*   B—The Aid Pie*

Notes to Pie Chart B

Federal Loans include amounts awarded under the Stafford and PLUS programs, Perkins revolving fund, HEAL and other health professions loans.

Employer-paid Tuition includes federal and private cooperative education programs.

Federal Grants include Pell, SEOG, SSIG, CW-S, Paul Douglas Teacher Scholarships, Robert Byrd Honors Scholarships, ROTC, military educational bonuses, military academies, health profession programs, various graduate programs, and numerous smaller programs.

Veteran's Administration includes the GI Bill, VEAP, and various educational benefits to dependents of veterans.

College Resources include scholarships, the collegiate share of CW-S, non-subsidized student employment programs, loans from the colleges' own resources, and tuition remissions.

The States include the state share of federal programs, state grant programs and special loan programs that supplement Stafford and PLUS.

Other categories are self-explanatory.

*Figures are all estimated for the 95/96 academic year based on FY95 Budget requests.

LOOKING TO THE FUTURE

Our next point. Paying for college isn't a one-year, one-shot deal. You must think in terms of this year's costs, next year's costs, and the following year's costs. If tuition charges strain you now, how desperate are you going to be by the time you are a Junior? Or four years from now when you'll be a Senior, and graduating? You must have a sense of all the external factors that can come into play, those that assist you in your effort to meet educational expenses, as well as those that impede you.

How far out should your crystal ball extend? Four years, if you plan on a baccalaureate. Six years or more, if a graduate or professional degree is your objective. Ten years or more, if yours is a family with several college-bound students.

A lot will happen during the next four, six, or ten years. Some of it is uncertain, but a few trends stand out. You should be conscious of these trends and make them part of your continuous, long-range planning. Here are the most important ones:

TREND A: COLLEGE COSTS TO INCREASE FASTER THAN INFLATION

No sunshine here. But it's a hard fact and must be considered. Why do tuition hikes continue to outpace inflation?

- **Higher education is labor intensive.** For this reason, technological gain does not have as great an impact on "productivity" in the academic world as it does in the industrial world. Great teaching, as Socrates and Plato knew, comes from conversation between two inquiring minds. College students cannot be turned out like Model Ts. More teachers are needed.

  Within this larger trend, there are some smaller ones that bear close watching. For instance, in certain fields, such as engineering, computer science and geology, industry provides much higher salary scales than college departments. In consequence, graduate students are turning to industry and not to teaching, and professors now teaching are moving in increasing numbers from campus to corporate suites. To fight this trend, colleges must continue to offer much more attractive salary packages. Meanwhile, the faculty shortages in these popular areas result in tougher admission standards for students seeking to major in these fields, more crowded classrooms, and less individualized attention.

- **State support of higher education is lagging behind costs.** The nation's public universities depend on state appropriations for 60% or more of their support. When state appropriations cannot keep pace with rising costs, the universities and community colleges must compensate by raising in-state tuitions and sky-rocketing their out-of-state charges (it's okay to slip it to out-of-staters: they pay taxes and vote somewhere else).

- **Computermania.** College after college is grabbing headlines by announcing that every student will be equipped with a personal computer. These computers must be linked by networks and supported by main frames. They need wiring, cooling, programming, maintenance people, a training staff, and what have you. All this costs money.

- **Technology.** If colleges are to be on the leading edge of technology, they must have the latest in laboratories, research equipment, machinery. Most of them don't have it now. Getting it will cost billions.

- **Deferred maintenance.** Leaky roofs. Crumbly foundations. Cracking asphalt. Inaccessible pipes. Paint jobs. Ivy won't hold up the walls forever. Our campuses need over $70 billion in repairs.

- **Fuel costs.** These are, proportionally, a far greater burden on college budgets than on family budgets. Old buildings, drafty halls, and a student population that overloads the circuits with electric gadgets ranging from hair dryers to popcorn poppers to VCRs to home computers keep the meters spinning.

- **The Robin Hood syndrome.** Collegiate student aid budgets, with very few exceptions, can no longer meet the financial need of all students. The common solution: Raise tuition charges through the roof; those who can pay will then, in effect, subsidize those who can't. At some of our nation's pricier schools, about 15% of each student's tuition goes toward scholarships for students with financial need. Saint Louis University, for example, recently raised tuition by 8% but increased its financial aid budget by 17%. Along these same lines, undergraduate tuition often subsidizes the education of graduate students, especially in the social sciences and humanities where grant money is increasingly scarce.

- **The declining prime age student population.** Through 1997, the number of people reaching college age will continue to decline. While some colleges have been able to make up the difference by enrolling increasing numbers of nontraditional students, others have not. At these less fortunate schools, fixed costs—plant, maintenance, tenured faculty salaries—are spread among fewer paying customers. To remain solvent, each student is asked to contribute more through higher tuitions.
- **Increased administration costs.** Red tape is rapidly encircling the nation's colleges and universities. Assistant and Associate Deans are everywhere, providing academic support, institutional support, and student services. College officials say these personnel costs are necessary and result from the need to administer many new student services and respond to increasingly complex, state and federal education regulations. But when you look at the numbers—a 61% increase in support staff over a ten-year period, as compared to a 5.9% increase in full-time faculty members during the same period—more schools might follow the example of Lehigh, Middlebury, Dartmouth, the State University of New York, and San Diego State, all of which have eliminated dozens of jobs and millions of dollars from their administrative budgets. Welcome to the real world!
- **Price vs. quality.** While many people are growing uneasy over rising tuition costs, some of the nation's most competitive colleges have found the reverse to be true. These schools feel that many people judge quality by price; the greater the price tag, the higher the perceived quality, and the greater the applicant pool. Admission reports bear out this belief. Accordingly, some schools seem to raise their tuition at the same rate as their competitors regardless of projected budgets.
- **Price fixing.** For 35 years, many of the nation's most prestigious schools met each spring to share information about the amount of aid they would offer to their common (overlapping) applicants. Their goal was to come to an agreement about the abilities of these students to pay tuition bills. The schools felt this exchange was in the best interest of all involved. It allowed students to select a college based on academic needs and educational quality rather than economics. It also prevented bidding wars for the top students, which in turn, preserved financial aid funds for truly needy students. Families, however, saw it differently. In their eyes, this process denied them all the aid to which they were entitled. More importantly, it assumed they were unable to make decisions about what is and is not important to them in selecting a college. If price is a factor in that decision, then it's the family's right to have a choice of aid packages.

Does this all sound like price fixing? For two years, the Justice Department investigated possible anti-trust violations (including the possibility of collusion over tuition increases and the setting of faculty salaries). The charges have since been dropped, and a settlement negotiated. It is as follows: Participating colleges *may* agree to offer only need-based financial aid and prohibit merit scholarships; they *may* agree on the principles of need analysis; and they *may* submit information to a third party auditor after aid awards have been made, so the third party can analyze whether the awards are in compliance with their agreement. Meanwhile, participating colleges *may not* discuss the actual aid packages awarded to mutual applicants. They *may not* agree on the mix of grants and loans that make up an aid package. And they *may not* discuss prospective tuition rates or faculty salaries. Before a school may participate in this sharing of information, it must agree to admit students without regard to financial need, and it must promise to meet the full need of every admitted student. Unfortunately, many colleges are not in the financial position to make these promises, so the effectiveness of the "Overlap Group" is greatly diminished and the predicted bidding wars have in fact begun (see Trend C).

7

- **Comparison shopping.** Fact. Colleges must compete for students. As students and parents become more sophisticated shoppers, they expect more for their money. Colleges must provide ample sports and recreational facilities for both men and women. They must maintain adequate levels of campus security, health care facilities (complete with resident psychologists, psychiatrists and drug/alcohol abuse counselors), and extensive career placement offices. Rooms must be wired for computers, hair driers and stereos. And dining halls must accommodate a variety of dietary requirements. As some of the above paragraphs point out, all of this costs money. The irony is, that the very people who complain about rising college costs are in part responsible for urging tuitions upward.
- **College is not as expensive as most people think.** Actually, we have a bit of good news. In a recent poll, students placed the average cost (tuition and fees) of a private four-year institution at $3,000 higher than actual tuition, and the average cost of a public four-year institution at nearly $5,000 higher than actual tuition. When you think about it, even today, with the cost of a private college averaging nearly $19,500, students are getting a pretty good deal. For what amounts to $80/day, the student is provided with a room (including heat, water and electricity), three meals a day, professional health care, recreational facilities, a wide range of social and cultural activities, counseling services, career assistance, and an education. Even better, students pay only about $40/day for all of this at a public school.

TREND B: TUITION PRICE WALL

"Bennington Cuts Tuition, Reduces Staff and Eliminates Tenure" read a recent *New York Times* headline. Traditionally one of our nation's most expensive colleges, Bennington will undergo major restructuring to reduce tuition by 10% over the next five years. Other colleges are also "redesigning" and "re-engineering" to live within their means. With personnel costs making up nearly 70% of some school's budgets, what this really means is lots of layoffs, buyouts and early retirements. Is this a sign that with top colleges now costing over $25,000 per year we're finally hitting a price wall? Let's hope so! Otherwise, no matter how wise a financial aid consumer you become, private colleges may soon become unaffordable for most middle income families. According to the College Board, public colleges eat up about 16% of median family income; about the same percentage as in 1960. Private colleges, however, consume about 42% of median income, compared to 27% in 1960. After years of watching tuition go through the roof with very little consequence (other than cries of horror when the College Board releases its annual survey of college costs), we're finally seeing more articles that talk about what colleges are doing to keep costs in line. Unfortunately, some schools are accomplishing this by eliminating more esoteric courses, or even entire departments.

TREND C: BIDDING WARS

How do you feel about the car buying process? Do you feel as though every one else gets a better price? Or do you feel pretty confident that you've beaten the salesperson at his or her own game? I personally will do just about anything to avoid haggling over a price, and feel very badly that some financial aid administrators have been put in a position where even the wealthiest parents and students feel as though it's their right to negotiate for better aid packages. Unfortunately, the process of awarding financial aid based entirely on "need" is now more of an ideal than an actuality as more and more schools use tuition discounts (or "merit scholarships") to meet their recruiting goals. This flexibility in awarding aid has led to a deal making mentality which truly has the potential to corrupt the equalizing powers of higher education. As The *Washington Post* recently editorialized, those who are more sophisticated or better advised will haggle while the less connected or less confident will not. This cleavage between the "information haves" and "information have-nots" is doubly dangerous when located at the very gateway to education-based upward mobility. We'll have more to say about negotiating aid packages in Chapters 7 and 9.

TREND D: YOUR FICKLE UNCLE SAM

Uncle Sam is the main dispenser of student aid. But Uncle changes his programs every year; sometimes, twice a year. His programs expand and shrink in dollar volume. Money that is authorized may never be appropriated. Money that is appropriated can be rescinded. Eligibility for the programs is as variable as the dollars. In year A you may be eligible. In year B you are out. In year C you are in again—but for a different amount of aid.

This instability is not limited to dollars. It also extends to their delivery. Forms may be late. Deep questions must be resolved on such matters as how to verify selective service registration. The academic year may have started, the dollars appropriated, but the machinery for delivering the dollars is still being tuned.

To complicate matters, the United States faces a $255 billion budget deficit this year. While the deficit has certainly gotten smaller since the Reagan/Bush years, Uncle still needs all the tax dollars he can get. As a result, Congress keeps passing new tax laws to reduce personal finance games as a way to create tuition money. The Administration keeps proposing higher education rule changes to find ways to prevent low life from abusing the system (For example, defaults on student loans cost nearly $1 billion last year!). And finally, Uncle's giving less money to the states, resulting in similar instability at that level as well.

Uncle needs close watching. To watch him intelligently, you should develop a working acquaintance with "authorizations," "appropriations," "budget reconciliations," "Federal Regulations," and "rescissions." Better still, read the new edition of this book which comes out every fall. We'll do the Uncle-watching for you.

TREND E: COLLEGES WANT YOU

There is a sunny side to the declining student population. Colleges now want you, more than ever before. Your parents may still think in terms of great college selectivity, however, for all but about 100 schools, selectivity is out the window. The operating word is "survival." Today, over 90% of all students are accepted by one of their top two college choices. The seller's market has become a buyer's market. It widens your opportunity to shop wisely and well. And the more marketable you are—good grades, leadership, musical talent, athletic ability—the more college-sponsored financial aid opportunities you will find.

One caution: Under pressure to recruit students, college materials have become slicker in execution. There is a greater willingness, on the part of colleges, to tell you about their own strengths and their competitors' weaknesses. In their efforts to attract the best and the brightest, colleges have used advertising, direct mail, and phone solicitation. Many have even turned to professional filmmakers (at $30,000 - $50,000 a shot) for a more direct, emotional sales pitch. Some schools spend as much as $800 per freshman actually enrolled.

Don't be too critical of schools for these practices. Their survival may be at stake. But do raise your consumer guards and evaluate collegiate mass-marketing techniques with the same objectivity and skepticism you normally reserve for television advertisements and mass-marketing techniques originating from other sources.

TREND F: TUITION AID IN RETURN FOR SERVICES

The nation needs more teachers. How can it stimulate interest in this field yet continue to pay teachers minuscule wages? Easy. Provide loans to prospective teachers. If the recipients actually go into teaching, the loans are "forgiven." But, if the recipients decide, after graduation, that working in a bike shop would be more rewarding than teaching math, the loan money must be repaid, with interest. Federal and state versions of this program have become common. Also expect to see the concept extended to any and all fields that can be stimulated by educational incentives that are cheaper than paying a competitive salary.

9

Recent surveys show our nation also needs to stimulate its social conscience; materialism is on the rise. Accordingly, the Administration pushed hard for its National Service Bill (resulting in AmeriCorps). Even though its scope is small, the attention it's getting should spur support for the dozens of state and local agencies (as well as the colleges) who are starting their own "volunteer "programs. More will be said about this kind of tuition assistance in Chapters 10, 11 and 15.

TREND G: GROWING CASH FLOW PROBLEMS—GROWING CASH FLOW HELP

When tuitions rise faster than available student aid, parents and students must make up the difference. But this is not a "vive la difference" to be cheered. It is a nasty cash flow problem that can and will grow worse with each passing year. A cash flow problem, in case you don't understand, comes about when you have the money to pay the bills, but the money is not "liquid." It is tied up in assets like your house, and you certainly don't want to sell your house just to pay the college bills.

But take heart. Problems create solutions. Financial innovators are coming up with plans that will help with the cash flow without requiring you to place a "For Sale" sign in front of the family castle. For instance, several states have raised money on the tax-exempt bond market for no other purpose than to make low-interest college loans. Banks and brokerage houses have credit lines that permit flexible borrowing against your home equity. Colleges themselves are becoming lenders, providing long-term loans at adjustable interest rates.

A lot is going on. And, we'll cover it at the precise point in this book when you throw up your hands and say, "We can't do it. No Way." We figure this will come around Chapter 7.

TREND H: FINANCIAL PLANNERS TO THE RESCUE

Personal finance experts appear under many guises—stockbrokers, financial planners, bankers, accountants, and insurance people. Most of these people are bright, resourceful professionals who can be of genuine help in the college financing process. Unfortunately, some of them are good at planning only one thing—their own lucrative retirement. Before you enlist in any of their services, ask some questions. *Are they fee only planners or do they work on commission? About how much are you going to pay for their services? Do they have a minimum account size?* Fee only planners charge by the hour. While this may cost you more money in the short-run, fee only planners point out that their counterparts don't always have real incentives to provide you with totally unbiased service (i.e., some planners on commission will give you nothing but a glossy sales pitch for whatever products bring the largest commission). If at all possible, find out how much of the planner's income comes from each of four sources: commissions, fees you pay for their advice, fees you pay for them to manage your funds, and fees they receive from companies that pay them to sell their products. *What are their fields of expertise? Their investment strategies?* Your planner should be familiar with investment strategies of all types—traditional advice on retirement planning and estate planning is not necessarily compatible with sound college planning. Your advisor should be able to explain these possible conflicts and help you maximize all of your resources (while minimizing your tax consequences). And, your planner should be a good listener, keeping your comfort level in mind while helping you with your financial plan. *What is their prior work experience?* Did they get their start in law? Accounting? Insurance? A brokerage house? A college financial aid office? Charm school? *What are their professional credentials? How long have they been in business?* Do they still have ties to an insurance company or brokerage house? Are they with an established company such as IDS Financial Services (a division of American Express) or Waddell & Reed? Have they been certified by a reputable group such as The Institute of Certified Financial Planners or The National Endowment for Financial Education (formerly The College for Financial Planning)? *Is the planner providing you with a service you can't get from your accountant or your lawyer?* There is no sense in paying for the same service twice. **Finally, ask for references: Reputable planners don't want to be confused with the scam artists and will be only too happy to oblige.**

For more information, or to find a planner in your area:
- American Society of CLU and ChFC (insurance agents and planners with an insurance orientation) — 800/392-6900
- Institute of Certified Financial Planners — 800/282-7526
- National Association of Personal Financial Advisors (fee-only planners) — 800/366-2732
- International Association for Financial Planning — 800/945-4237
- American Institute of Certified Public Accountants (Personal Financial Specialists, or planners who are CPAs) — 800/862-4272

TREND I: FASCINATION WITH EXCELLENCE

Major studies have aroused public opinion about the decline of excellence in elementary and secondary schools. Nearly every solution suggested requires tons of money. Lengthen the school day. Lengthen the school year. Pay some teachers more than others. Pay all teachers more. Make everyone wear uniforms. Build single sex schools. Plug a computer into every socket. Put a computer in every home. Increase spending on the arts. Decrease spending on the arts. Not all solutions will be adopted. But some will, and money will flow. For example, the "Goals 2000: Educate America Act" will get $100 million in its first year. The Administration is asking for $700 million in year two , and another billion in year three. Most of this money is slated to go to the states, which in turn will award money to local school systems. Which school systems get the money? Those that agree to follow the Goals 2000 blueprint for educating children and adopt the "voluntary" academic standards being written for math, science, history, geography, foreign languages and the arts.

While a nation of literate, math whizzes sounds wonderful, in a finite economy, that money must come from somewhere. Most likely, it will come from money that otherwise might have gone to financing your higher education.

But again, there is a sunny side. The enshrining of excellence legitimates the use of academic scholarships, on the part of colleges, to attract high-performance students. Expect continued growth in such awards.

TREND J: A COLLEGE EDUCATION STILL PAYS

A college education will prepare you for a fulfilling life — through broader cultural awareness, deeper knowledge, greater self-confidence, sounder health, richer pleasures, keener citizenship and vastly expanded resources for personal happiness.

If philosophical reasons aren't enough, and we've already mentioned the reported rise in materialism among college bound students, you'll be pleased to learn that college still helps you earn more money. Here are some recent figures from the US Bureau of the Census (adjusted for inflation). Please note: These are averages; women should subtract about 25% , and men should add about 25% to get a more realistic idea of what you can really expect to earn! (With great restraint, the author reserves comment on this income differential until Chapter 22.)

Highest Education Completed	Average Annual Income
High School	$14,546
College	$28,578
Master's	$38,114
Professional	$67,003

Chapter 2
Common Myths &
Misconceptions & Mistakes

Practically everyone we know equates the search for monetary help for college with a search for scholarships. Get rid of that belief quickly! And repeat after us three times: To obtain financial aid, sophisticated families:

- Present the family's situation for need analysis in the most favorable terms legally allowed.
- Apply to all the major assistance programs for which they are eligible.
- Apply early, accurately and honestly.
- Select colleges that are most likely to present them with a good aid package.
- When appropriate, discuss with the financial aid administrator the possibility of improving the aid that was offered.
- Become knowledgeable of favorable options—commercial or otherwise—for financing educational expenses not covered by aid awards.

These steps can be worth thousands of dollars. Any other approach will make you the unknowing looking for the unfindable. You will gain nothing, while paying out plenty—in wasted time and money. Now read this short chapter on the myths, misconceptions, fables and folklore that envelop the financial aid field. And remember: You don't profit from these beliefs; only the people who keep them alive do.

WON'T A SCHOLARSHIP REPLACE MY MONEY?

Most people believe that scholarships will put money in their pocket. Example: You have been assessed a $5,000 per year contribution to College X, a school that costs more than that to attend. One lucky day, you win a $1,000 scholarship. You now say your contribution will be $4,000. Right? Wrong. Your contribution will still be $5,000. The college takes the $1,000 and incorporates it into your financial aid package where it may replace a loan or a work opportunity or a grant that the college had planned on using to help you. The colleges have another option for handling your award. They can decide that the scholarship increases your available resources. Instead of a $5,000 contribution, you are now capable of making a $6,000 contribution. **Either way, the scholarship will help pay your college bill but it will not reduce your share of the bill.**

If that is so, you may ask, then why do clubs and organizations work so hard to raise scholarship money to help a particular student? The answer: They are not familiar with college financial aid packaging techniques. If they were, all that money raised by candy bar sales and church suppers would go to a different purpose.

Another question. Why do colleges urge students to find scholarships? Every college catalogue suggests that students check with their guidance office or visit their public library. The answer: The scholarship you bring to the college will, in effect, free some of the college's money that had been earmarked to help you. It can now use that money to help another student. What results, in fact, is that the scholarship won by Student A will actually benefit Student B. This may not have been the donor's intention, but it is a generous act and should not go unnoticed. Remember: It's only the money that goes to the other student. You, the winner, retain the honor and prestige of having won the scholarship.

LOOKING FOR SPECIAL SCHOLARSHIPS

Every day we get letters from people who give us their age, sex, race, career intentions, physical condition and personal finance data and then ask "is there a special scholarship for me?" These letters sadden us, because we know the writers haven't followed the normal route for getting financial aid.

Here is what we reply, "Please don't waste your time looking for a special award for a (black, white, green) 35-year-old, seeking to return to the labor force as a sorcerer's apprentice. Most financial aid comes from Uncle Sam, your state, or your college and is based on financial need and student status. If college costs more than your assessed contribution, you are eligible for financial aid. Your age, sex, race and career ambitions have nothing to do with it."

Even if you do find a "special scholarship" source, remember, there's a big difference between being eligible and winning. For example, your odds of winning a 4-H award (approximately 300 awards and 500,000 HS seniors as members), are only 1670:1. To increase your chances, you could purchase a one-week old piglet, feed it 20 times a day until it weighs 1700 pounds. Then rent a forklift and a truck, take it to the state fair, and hope it wins a blue ribbon in the heavy hog competition. This might improve your odds of winning to 20 or 30 to 1. But what about the costs of raising a 1700 pound porker?

Our advice: Go the traditional financial aid route (Parts II and III) first. Then, if you have a lot of time and nothing else to do, and you need practice writing letters and you feel you must help the Postal Service stay in the black, start looking for a "special scholarship." You may even find one.

UNCLAIMED SCHOLARSHIPS

Q. I have read that millions of dollars in scholarship funds go unclaimed every year. Is this true?

A. If you believe this, you probably also believe you'll win that $100 million lottery (at odds of 9.6 million to 1). Seriously, a few dollars in college aid does go unclaimed, but according to most financial aid professionals, the millions you hear about are unused employee tuition benefits. See below.

SCHOLARSHIPS FROM CORPORATIONS & FOUNDATIONS

Q. I have heard that big corporations offer a lot of scholarships.

A. Many do—to the children of their employees. If your mom works for NIKE or Black & Decker, you might get help. If your dad works in the neighborhood barbershop—forget it! Some corporations have awards for other than their employees' children. These are usually administered by colleges which in turn select the recipients. You can't apply for them directly.

Q. What about foundations?

A. Mainly, they help students at the doctoral or post-doctoral level. There is also some money for the college-bound and undergraduates. But that money usually has very narrow local restrictions, e.g., for students in Teenytiny County. Normally, such localized foundation grants are well publicized on the school bulletin board and in the local paper. But if they aren't and you don't want to miss any of these opportunities, then spend some time in the public library with a reference book called *Foundation Grants to Individuals*.

COMPUTERIZED SCHOLARSHIP SEARCHES

If you need information on federal or state student aid, don't pay a computer service. You can learn all you need to know from this book or the free pamphlets that Uncle Sam and your state government hand out.

If you need information on student aid offered by the colleges to which you are applying, don't pay a computer service. The college catalogue will tell you what you need to know.

If you need information on scholarships offered by your employer or church, don't pay a computer service. Ask your boss or minister.

If you need information on local scholarships, don't pay a computer service. Check the high school bulletin board.

Most experts agree; computerized scholarship services are not likely to be of much help in your search for private aid. At their very best, they might provide you with a few leads, as opposed to actual dollars; but we've heard too many horror stories of families being duped out of $250 processing fees to recommend this route to anyone (unless, of course, your state, or college, or high school has a search service you can use for free, or you take advantage of a low cost offer, like the one in *Need A Lift* – see Chapter 13 for ordering information). Concrete Example: In New York, the Better Business Bureau gave 20 of 21 scholarship search services an "Unsatisfactory" rating. Nine other operations had closed before the bureau could contact them. Can you say "fraud"?

TRUSTS, GIFTS AND OTHER DEVICES CAN BE HAZARDOUS TO YOUR COLLEGE BILLS

Many people can't accept the fact they are in a higher tax bracket than their children. They will shift assets from themselves to their offspring, thinking the income from these assets will then be taxed at a much lower rate. Such transfers used to take the simple form of a deposit into junior's savings account. Then, people became more sophisticated and used all sorts of income-shifting Trusts which had to be constructed with the help of lawyers and accountants whose fees could run upwards of $1,000.

Then, Congress passed new tax laws and all this maneuvering went for naught. Investment income in excess of $1,200 for children under 14 is now taxed at the parents rate, regardless of its source. Furthermore, the tax rates for trusts is now higher than the tax rates for most families. What was left for families to do? Pay financial planners even more money to tell them how to get out of their current fiscal mess.

In short, some schemes devised by financial planners should carry a big red warning label that says, "This Device May Be Hazardous To Your College Bills." You'll understand why after you have read Chapters 7 and 8.

READING THE WRONG REFERENCES

Everybody knows that Consumer Reports' Income Tax Guide takes a somewhat different slant to its subject than publications from the IRS. Consumer Reports' objective is to show you ways to save on taxes while the IRS seeks to extract the last drop of blood. You may value the IRS guide for its mechanical instructions, but not for its substantive advice on holding on to more of your money.

It's the same with paying-for-college guides. Before you purchase one or read one, make sure you know the guide's origin. Is it written from the viewpoint of those who pay the money (parents or students)? Is it written by those who get the money (colleges and collegiate organizations)? Or is it written by those who give the money (Uncle Sam and the states)? The guides may treat the same subject, but their treatment could be many dollars (your dollars) apart.

READING OLD REFERENCES

In student financial aid, any reference older than one year is out of date. If you use an older reference, you will be badly misled with regard to loan sources, interest rates, aid eligibilities, grants size, saving techniques, government regulations, and college costs.

This wisdom is especially true for students starting school after the 1994/95 academic year. The passage of the Higher Education Amendments of 1992 means changes in nearly every federal student aid program, beginning with the way Uncle Sam determines your eligibility for these programs Also, the current Administration has a very ambitious education agenda, and is promising "major reforms" in student aid policy. With lots of kinks still being worked out, it's important to stay current!

Part II
The Fundamentals of Financial Aid

Chapter 3
Using this Guide

The sequence of topics in the rest of this guide parallels the steps you should take in your quest for college financing. First, you must define your monetary need and second, you must learn how to finance that need.

We ask that you do not skip to the resources listed at end of the book and begin firing off appeals for help. Chances are good that it will be an unproductive way to spend your time and the time of the kind organizations offering assistance.

Instead, start at the beginning.

In Part II of this book you will learn the special vocabulary of financial aid. You will meet the players in the financial aid game, and you will develop an understanding of their roles and interests and come to appreciate that these interests may not always be the same as yours. Also, in Part II, you will learn how to calculate your family contribution—the amount of money your family is judged capable of contributing to college costs. We will guide you through the entire aid application process and show you how to take charge of each step along the way.

Why is taking charge important?
1. It increases your eligibility for aid.
2. It enhances your chances of receiving all the aid to which you are entitled.
3. It improves the composition of your award, meaning more grants and fewer loans.
4. It gives you a major advantage over those who enter the process passively, without understanding what is being done to them.
5. It gives you a gargantuan advantage over those who drift through the process in complete confusion.
6. It gives you an infinite advantage over those who don't enter the process at all.

In Part III, you move from the fundamentals to more advanced approaches. You become a financial aid whiz who masters all the moves in the financial aid game—college selection, personal finance techniques, and tax strategies. You will learn the best moves for each of two different situations: (1) when college entrance is approaching fast and (2) when college is still years away.

In Part IV, you will meet the major money sources—the colleges, Uncle Sam, and the states. They are the dispensers of billions of dollars. By getting to know their programs well, you will not overlook a single penny that is due you.

Part V introduces you to two major alternatives for financing college costs—your boss, and the US military. The suggestions offered may not be to your liking, but you should know about them and consider or reject them at this point in the decision process.

Part VI groups special opportunities. You've already had the meat and potatoes course. Now you are looking for the cake or maybe just the frosting. You'll find sections here for the bright and for the career-oriented, for the athlete and for the graduate student, for minorities and for women, and for the handicapped. One or more of these special opportunities are bound to fit your situation and round out your meal. The tips at the end of Part VI bring together many of the ideas and suggestions developed earlier at greater length. Use these tips as a review.

There is no Part VII. But if there was, it would be an award ceremony where we present you with the title of "Financial Aid Guru."

Chapter 4
Definitions & Players

Grants and Scholarships are aid awards that do not have to be repaid. They are gifts. Some scholarships, though not all, will require you to perform a service. The recipient of a band scholarship, for instance, will have to dress up in a funny costume complete with spats, march around a football field, and blow into a piccolo or tuba whenever the college so directs.

Loans are sums of money that must be repaid. To qualify as financial aid, loans must carry an interest charge that is lower than prevailing commercial rates. They must also offer favorable repayment provisions. An example of favorable repayment provisions: the Stafford Loan. Borrowers do not start paying interest on the loan nor do they have to retire any of the principal until six months after completing their studies.

Work counts as financial aid when employment is arranged for you through the financial aid office. Earnings from work you found yourself are not included as part of financial aid. Such earnings are added to the sum you are judged capable of contributing to college costs.

Enrollment Status impacts on aid eligibility. To qualify for some federal student aid as well as state aid and money from the college, you must be at least a half-time student. Half-time is generously defined. It consists of six semester or quarter hours per academic term for schools on the semester, quarter, or trimester system; 12 semester hours or 18 quarter hours per school year for schools that use a credit hour system; or 12 clock hours a week for schools that use clock hours to measure course programs.

Under this system, a $1,000 award for a full-time student becomes a $750 award for a three-quarter-time student (one majoring in the waltz?) and $500 for a half-time student. Even programs authorized to award financial aid to less-than-half-time students, only do so if there are extra funds (i.e., if the money will not be taken from someone else who needs it). This scenario is not likely. **A tip:** If you are a part-time student and wish to qualify for aid, take one more course each semester.

Accreditation is a process that ensures the school's programs maintain at least a minimum level of quality. Make sure the school you plan to attend has been accredited by a nationally recognized accreditation association. Not only do you not want to waste your tuition dollars getting a worthless education, but students who attend a non-accredited school will not qualify for federal or state student aid.

Program Eligibility is the latest code phrase in the Administration's effort to eliminate student aid fraud and abuse. What you need to know is this: An educational program must contain a minimum number of clock hours to be considered an "eligible program." Also, students who enroll in programs that are shorter than one academic year are eligible for less federal assistance. Finally, schools that receive most of their funding from federal student aid programs are immediately suspect. Students working toward an associate, bachelor, professional or graduate degree need not worry much about "program eligibility." Students looking at proprietary schools (for a two month study, for example, of computer repair) should take heed. Most student aid fraud takes place in vocational programs of less than two years, and Uncle Sam is trying his best to separate the wheat from the chaff (shaft?).

THE 1ST PLAYER—THE STUDENT

Students may see themselves as "A" students or "C" students, as freshmen or juniors, as jocks or dweebs, as hot or not.

Financial aid programs have their own classification system that defines students by dependency status. They are either independent students or dependent students.

A dependent student is one who is at least partially dependent on his or her parents for support. The income and assets of both student and parent are used to develop the amount a family must contribute to college costs.

An independent student is not dependent on parental support. Only the student's income and assets (and that of any relevant spouse) are evaluated to determine the contribution to college costs. An independent student may also be classified as a dislocated worker as defined below ("The 2nd Player—The Parents").

To be considered independent, under federal regulations, a student must meet one of the following conditions:

1. Be 24 years of age by December 31 of the award year (e.g., December 31, 1995 for the 1995/96 award year).
2. Be an orphan or ward of the court.
3. Be a veteran of the Armed Services.
4. Have legal dependents other than a spouse.
5. Be married.
6. Be a professional student, or a graduate student.
7. Be judged independent by the financial aid administrator based on documented unusual circumstances.

Establishing independence usually gives you an advantage: By not having to include parental income and assets on your financial aid application forms, your college contribution will most likely be lower and that will result in more student aid.

To preserve scarce aid funds, most states and almost all colleges have gone beyond the federal test to impose additional restrictions on your declaration of independence. These include written proof that your parents (or even grandparents) cannot provide any support whatsoever. This is especially true for students who are "independent" according to Uncle Sam's definition, but who have moved back home with mom and dad to save some money.

THE 2ND PLAYER—THE PARENTS

Parents may be sweet, loving, caring, supportive role models. The financial aid process doesn't care. Its main interest: Are they married, separated, divorced? Is there a stepparent around who can foot the bill?

Here is the impact of marital status on financial aid:

Both Parents Are Alive and Married to Each Other. The income and assets of both parents are fair pickings for the financial aid computer.

Parents Are Divorced Or Separated. Financial aid forms are interested in the income and assets of the parent with whom the student lived for the majority of the twelve months preceding the date of the application. The form is not interested in the other parent.

A Parent Remarries. If the parent with whom the student lived the greater part of the twelve months preceding the date of the application remarries, the stepparent automatically assumes partial responsibility for the student. His or her income and assets are evaluated for a contribution to college costs as though he or she were a natural parent.

These rules apply to federal aid and, generally, to state aid. The colleges, when they decide how to dispense their own money, are not bound by these rules. They can probe deeply into the resources of the divorced and absent parent who got off scot-free under federal regulations.

The financial aid process also cares about the parent's (or independent student's) employment status. In determining a family's eligibility for financial aid, financial aid administrators are encouraged to give special consideration to "dislocated workers." For example, they may recalculate family contribution using expected income, rather than prior year income. If you fall into this category, it's your responsibility to let the financial aid administrator know!

> **Parent (or Independent Student) is a Dislocated Worker.** This category is defined by individual state agencies in accordance with Title III of the Job Training Partnership Act. To see if a parent qualifies, check with your state's employment service. In general, however, "dislocated worker" refers to an individual who has been:
> 1. Fired or laid off (or has received notice of termination) OR
> 2. Laid off as part of a permanent factory closing (or one that will soon close) OR
> 3. Unemployed for a long period with little chance for reemployment in the same or similar occupation in the area where he or she resides OR
> 4. Self-employed (including farmers) but is now unemployed because of a natural disaster or poor economic conditions within the community.

THE 3RD PLAYER—THE COLLEGES

We'll say a lot more about colleges in Chapter 9. At this time, you should know that colleges can be classified as either private or public.

Private colleges can be more innovative in developing attractive college financing schemes and tuition assistance programs. They are not as circumscribed by red tape as are tax-supported schools.

Private colleges also have more latitude in how to spend their money. Again, it's their money, not the taxpayer's (this also means they're apt to pry more deeply into your family's finances as they try to decide who is most deserving of limited aid funds).

Public colleges, being tax-supported, are usually less expensive. As a general rule, students seldom pay more then 30% of actual tuition costs. The state pays the balance.

Also, public colleges have two sets of fee structures: a lower one for state residents and a higher one for out-of-staters. At one time, it was easy to establish state residency to qualify for the lower rate. Today, it's getting difficult. Most states have erected elaborate defense structures staffed with obedient public servants whose efficiency often appears to be judged in direct proportion to the number of residency denials issued.

One more thing. Private and public colleges have no great love for one another. The lack of affection is rooted in money. The privates resent the subsidies that permit the public schools to offer lower tuitions. They would love to end this "unfair competition" by qualifying for subsidies of their own. Moreover, they see their own turf invaded when public schools, not fully sated by subsidies, seek funds from philanthropies that let them get around the inflexible expenditure guidelines imposed by the states. The public schools, for their part, resent the infusion of state money into private college coffers, especially if the state's commitment to its public schools has diminished. Furthermore, they're tired of all the bureaucracy. Some of the wealthier state schools have tried to escape the red tape by privatizing themselves.

Some of this hostility ends when the two must present a united front (strength in numbers) to fend off repeated efforts to slash the federal education budget.

THE 4TH PLAYER—THE NEED ANALYSIS SERVICES

Before a college can consider you for aid, it must know how much you can pay. The family that can pay $10,000 won't be eligible for as much as the family that can spare only $1,000.

Determining how much you can pay, without becoming a burden to your neighbors, is called **Need Analysis.** The job is performed by a giant computer using data you provide on a longish form called the Free Application for Federal Student Aid (FAFSA). Uncle Sam has contracts with four application processing systems to send data from the FAFSAs to this giant computer (also known as the central processing system). They are: the College Board's College Scholarship Service (Princeton, NJ), the American College Testing Program (Iowa City, IA), the Pennsylvania Higher Education Assistance Agency (Harrisburg, PA), and the Education Department's own processor, ED Application Processor (Iowa City, Iowa). Much more will be said about the FAFSA in Chapters 6, 7 and 10. Here we'll just summarize the mechanics of needs analysis so you know which computer to blame for each delay you experience!

1. You send your completed Free Application for Federal Student Aid (FAFSA) to one of the four application processors mentioned above.
2. The application processor transmits your data to the central processing system.
3. The central processor evaluates your family finances and spits out your "Expected Family Contribution" (EFC).
4. The central processor transmits your EFC back to the application processor.
5. The application processor incorporates your EFC into a multi-part eligibility report called a Student Aid Report (SAR).
6. The application processor sends you a copy of your SAR.
7. The application processor transmits your application data to any schools you designate on your FAFSA.
8. The application processor transmits your application data to the state higher education agency you designate on your FAFSA.

Because the formula used to calculate your EFC is mandated by Uncle Sam, it is known as the Federal Methodology. As you can see from the above data flow, all EFCs are calculated by the same computer (which is actually invisible to the student), so you gain nothing by submitting your FAFSA to one application processor rather than another. So why are there four different processors? Partly to spread out the work load. But also because some states and colleges like to have additional knowledge about your family's finances to determine eligibility for their own programs, especially since the FAFSA no longer includes basic questions about your family's assets like "How much is your home worth?" Processors, therefore, can package the FAFSA with an additional form to collect "supplemental material" to meet the needs of these, their real clients. The College Board calls its supplemental form the Financial Aid Form (FAF). You'll learn more about which forms to use in Chapter 6. Just remember, it's important to use the right one to make certain you're considered for every aid source possible.

THE FIFTH PLAYER—THE FINANCIAL AID ADMINISTRATOR

If money is water and you are a basin, the financial aid administrator is the faucet (Yes, I know. There will be letters from financial aid administrators who object to this metaphor. They would rather be likened to the valiant Hector rallying the warriors of ancient Troy. Well, maybe "faucet" is a bad word. Would "spigot" be better?). For the college-bound and those in college, the financial aid administrator can be the most important person on campus.

The FAA can take the family contribution cranked out by the need analysis services and—ouch—increase it or—hooray—reduce it. The FAA can draw on money under the college's control or certify the student's eligibility for money not under the school's direct control. The FAA can decide on the contents of the student's assistance package. Is it to be scholarships and grants that do not have to be repaid? Or will it all be in loans?

In short, the FAA is the final arbiter of how much the family must contribute to college costs and how much outside help, and of what kind, the family will receive. Get to know this player. He or she can make the difference between winning and losing.

Chapter 5
This You Must Understand

Ubi Est Mea? (Old Latin Proverb, Translation: Where is Mine?)

THE CONCEPT OF NEED

In a recent survey, The Council for Advancement and Support of Education (CASE) discovered that 49% of high school students believed they could not receive financial aid for an expensive private school if their parents could afford to send them to a state school. Thirty-three percent believed that almost all financial aid was set aside for minority students.

Of course, neither of these assumptions is true.

Most financial aid is based on the concept of "need." You cannot understand financial aid without understanding "need."

Need should never be confused with "needy."

Need is a number — nothing more, nothing less.

This is how to determine the need number:

Visualize three bars, Bar A, Bar B and Bar C. Bar A is the cost of attendance at the college of your choice. Bar B will represent your family's expected contribution to college costs, as determined by need analysis (see previous chapter). And Bar C is the amount of "outside" student aid you've received (e.g., private scholarships and veteran's benefits).

Bar A — the cost of attendance — is a variable. It will vary from college to college. It can even vary within one school, depending on your student status, the courses you take, how far away you live, etc. Bar B and Bar C, which, when added together make up your contribution, are constant (unless there is a drastic change in your family's situation). It doesn't matter where you plan to buy your education. The amount you must contribute from your own resources should be the same.

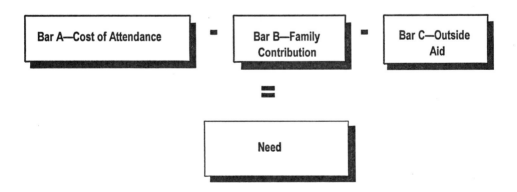

If Bar A is larger than Bar B and Bar C combined, you have financial need.

Let's illustrate this concept of need for a family judged capable of contributing $5,000 per year to college costs at three different colleges, College X which costs $19,000; College Y which costs $9,000; and College Z which costs $6,000:

Assuming the student has found a $1,000 scholarship, that family's need is $13,000 at College X; $3,000 at College Y; and a big fat $0 at College Z .

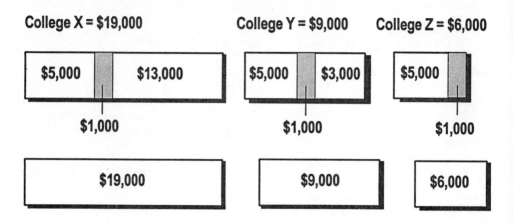

Casual Observation:

With a central processor and single, free application, it seems like Need Analysis should be much simpler now. It's as though Uncle Sam might finally succeed in reducing some of our paperwork!

Behind the Scenes:

Colleges that rely primarily on federal and state resources to make up financial aid packages seem satisfied with the current system of need analysis.

Students, who for the most part no longer have to pay to have their aid applications processed, seem satisfied with the current system of need analysis.

Unfortunately, colleges with a lot of institutional aid to distribute are a little frustrated by this new simplicity. Aid administrators at these schools feel the FAFSA does not gather enough information about a family's assets to calculate a family's true ability to pay. Accordingly, many no longer use the word "need" to describe the results obtained from processing the FAFSA. Instead, they refer to the results as a "family's eligibility for federal student aid." These schools then use an application form of their own (or the College Board's FAF) to gather additional information and determine a student's "need" for institutional funds. More will be said about how this affects the financial aid package in Chapter 6. For now, just be warned that at many schools, (especially heavily endowed, private schools) awarding aid based entirely on "need" (as determined by a uniform method of need analysis) is an ideal rather than a practice.

Finally: Don't think the elements that enter into the need calculation—the family contribution and the cost of college—are carved in stone. They are elastic. They can be stretched and squeezed. This is not the time to show you how to turn rock into play-doh. But it is time to let you know it can be done. In Chapter 7 you will find a plethora of ideas for stretching and squeezing.

Chapter 6
Taking Charge of the Link-Up Process

WHY TAKE CHARGE?

The admission and financial aid cycles operate on different schedules. You select colleges in the fall, apply during the winter, and get acceptance decisions in early spring.

The financial aid cycle, however, cannot be formally initiated until after the first of the year in which you plan to attend college (so the computers can be fed exact data on how much your family earned the previous year). You submit your aid application as soon as after January 1 as possible. Then you are kept in the dark for several months before you learn (1) how much you will have to contribute, (2) whether you have need (3) whether you qualify for need-based aid (4) and what your actual financial aid package will look like. Some years, students are asked to make their decision about what college to attend before they even receive their financial aid award letter.

If you want to assume your family contribution, once you learn what it is, will not cause you a cash-flow problem, and that your need will be met at whatever college you elect to attend, then you can trust the system and submit all your applications in the dark. You would then be like the good soldier who does what he is told, when he is told; who carries out all orders, even though he does not understand them.

But if you assume, realistically, that (1) your family contribution will impose a cash-flow burden, (2) your need will not be met in all cases or (3) if it is met, it may be met in a manner that may be financially burdensome to you, you cannot be a good soldier. You have to take charge of the process. In doing so, you protect your own interests. You guard against shocks and surprises. You allot adequate planning time. You improve your chances of having all your need met and met in an attractive manner. You may even succeed in lowering your family contribution and qualifying for more aid.

If you don't take charge, you will be as helpless as a jellyfish, bobbing in the waves, drifting where the tides take you. Eventually you will be soaked in brine and gobbled up by a killer whale.

What does all this mean? Let's translate these general statements into specifics to illustrate each point.

WHAT IS MEANT BY TAKING CHARGE?

Taking charge is not complex. You won't have to enroll in a leadership or muscle-building course or graduate from Infantry Officer Candidate School. All you have to do is read this chapter and the next and act on the advice they give you. The take-charge process has three elements:

1. **Learn the Money Numbers Ahead of Time.** Before you fill out the financial aid application you should know the size of your family contribution, the costs of the colleges of your choice, and the resulting amount of need you will have at each of these schools.

2. **Execute the Mechanics of the Application Process With Speed and Precision.** That's how you insure you'll be first in line for aid, before the "Sold Out" and "No Vacancy" signs light up.

3. **Know About Influence Points.** College selection, preparing yourself for need analysis, the speed and accuracy with which you apply, the evaluation of aid offers, financial aid administrators—these are all influence points. How you handle yourself as you approach these points will impact on your family contribution, aid eligibility, and size and composition of your aid award.

Your Objective	The Good Soldier	The Take-Charge Applicant
To guard against shock.	Won't learn of family contribution until late spring. Will be surprised by amount. Has little time to raise the money and may be forced to change college plans.	Knows from the start how much college will cost family. Has almost one year to figure out how to raise money.
Make sure size of aid package corresponds to need.	When selecting colleges, does not consider their ability to meet family's need fully.	Makes schools' ability to meet need part of college selection and application strategy.
Get an attractive aid package; one that's rich in grants and low on loans.	When selecting colleges, does not consider their ability to present an attractive aid package.	Makes schools' ability to present an attractive aid package part of college selection and application strategy.

KNOW THE MONEY NUMBERS AHEAD OF TIME

Let's begin with the first element of the take-charge process: Knowing the Money Numbers Ahead of Time. You do that by securing answers to three questions:

1. How much will our family be expected to contribute to college costs? For federal aid purposes, this will be a constant. For institutional aid, it may vary.
2. What are the annual costs of attendance at the college(s) of my choice? This is also a variable.
3. What's our need going to be at each college of my choice?

Once you have the answer to Question #3 — even if it's just an approximation — you can begin some sensible financial planning.

QUESTION #1: HOW MUCH WILL WE HAVE TO PAY?

Family Contribution is made up of four elements: the Parents' Contribution Income, the Parent's Contribution from Assets, the Student's Contribution from Income and the Student's Contribution from Assets (if you are an independent student, the Family Contribution will correspond to the Student's Contribution from Income and from Assets). Family contribution is calculated by Uncle Sam's central processor system and the need analysis services (see chapter 4).

To complicate matters, three different need analysis systems will be in operation for the 1995/96 school year.

All three systems operate on the same principle. They let you shelter some of your money for taxes, living expenses and retirement. Then they want what is left.

You should know that the income protection allowance — the money left to you for shelter, food, clothing, car operations, insurance and basic medical care — is based on the Department of Labor's "low budget standard." If you have gotten along on a low budget standard, the need analysis formula will fit you like a glove. But if you have become locked into a higher standard of living, with mortgage payments, fat utility bills, two cars, summer vacations, an occasional trip to the theater, and so on, the small allowance won't do you. It won't cover expenses. And your assessed family contribution will appear impossibly large!

Need Analysis System	Programs Served
Federal Methodology	1. All federal programs 2. Many state programs 3. Many collegiate programs 4. Many private donor programs
Simplified Need Test	Same as above
Institutional Methodology	1. Some state programs 2. Some collegiate programs 3. Some private donor programs

The Federal Methodology is the system that will, more than any other, impact on your eligibility for student aid. It should concern you the most. Incidentally, financial aid administrators say that 95% of parents and students don't understood need analysis. Can you imagine that? Plunking down $50,000 or $100,000 for an education and not knowing how your share of that cost is assessed! You, as one of our readers, will be among the 5% who know.

The Simplified Need Test may be used by families whose total parental adjusted gross incomes (or, in the case of independent students, the student and spouse's total adjusted gross incomes) are under $50,000 and who are eligible to file a 1040EZ, a 1040A, or who do not file a tax return at all. The simplified formula is essentially the same as the Federal Methodology with the following exception: It does not count assets in the family contribution calculation.

The Institutional Methodology is used primarily by higher priced colleges to determine eligibility for collegiate resources. The Institutional Methodology is essentially the same as the Federal Methodology, but with a few extra questions. For example, you will have to report the value of your home.

Now it's time to calculate the family contribution under the Federal Methodology. Dependent Students go to Appendix 1. Independent Students go to Appendix 2 or 3. The end product of your calculations won't match to the penny what the need analysis computer will determine. But the result will be in the ball park.

Here are some things to know before you start filling in the figures:

Dependent Students
- All income and tax data comes from the previous calendar year. If you start college in September 1995, the previous calendar year is 1994.
- All asset data is as of the date you submit the need analysis form.
- If your parents are divorced or separated, use the income and asset figures of the parent with whom you lived for the greater part of the twelve month period prior to the date of the application.
- If your parent has remarried, you must include your stepparent's income and asset information.

Independent Student
- All income and tax data comes from the previous calendar year. If you start college in September 1995, the previous calendar year is 1994.
- All asset data is as of the date you submit the need analysis form.

Dislocated Workers
If you, one of your parents, or your spouse is a dislocated worker (see Chapter 4), the financial aid administrator can make some adjustments in evaluating your expected

family contribution. For example, the FAA may recalculate your EFC using expected income (1995 for the 1995/96 award year) rather than previous year income.

An Important Point

Question. Why should I calculate the family contribution myself? The high school guidance office has a computer program that will make the calculation. I also understand that many college recruiters lug a portable computer around that will make the calculation.

Answer. Getting a number and accepting it casts you in the passive role colleges want you to assume in the financial aid application process. But getting that same number by calculating it yourself is part of the take-charge drill.

By making the calculation you will develop an appreciation of the formula, its components, and the weights assigned to each component. When you combine this knowledge with the "advanced information" provided in the next chapter, you will get ideas for rearranging family financial data so as to obtain the most favorable analysis possible. And that can be worth a lot of money. Also, an intimate knowledge of the formula's components will serve you well, later in the cycle, if you should have to discuss your aid award, and its calculation, with a financial aid administrator.

Institutional Methodology

The worksheets allow you to calculate your EFC under the Federal Methodology. To get an idea of what private colleges (and some out-of-state public colleges) will expect you to contribute, just add the equity in your home to the total value of your assets. Your family contribution should increase by an amount equal to about 5% of this equity. Also, if your parents are divorced, you should assume the private college will ask about the income of the parent whose information is not listed on the FAFSA.

If you want to prepare for the absolute worst, you should add in some other assets. For example, colleges with their own aid applications may ask for the current value of your retirement accounts (IRAs, Keoghs, 401 (k)s, single premiums) and question you about sibling assets (to make certain you're not hiding money in baby brother's bank account). Your family contribution will increase by about 5% of the total.

Again, the Federal Methodology determines eligibility for federal aid (and most state aid). It's a strict formula with little room for negotiation. The Institutional Methodology is used by many colleges to award need-based collegiate aid. The formula is not legislated so individual discretion can be wide and the room for negotiation sometimes great (depending on the policies of the school, and the desirability of the student).

Completely confused? One counselor from New Jersey lamented, "We now have two financial aid delivery systems, one for private colleges and one for public colleges."

QUESTION #2: HOW MUCH WILL COLLEGE COST?

OK. You have made an estimate of your family contribution. Now you need to know how much it will cost to attend the college of your choice. College costs and tuition are not synonymous. College costs—also known as "Cost of Attendance" or "Cost of Education" or "Student Expense Budget"—are an aggregate of six elements.

1. **Tuition and fees** are generally the same for all students.
2. **Book and supply** expenditures depend on the courses you select. You can purchase these items in the college store, in the community, or you can save some money and buy them in a used book emporium.
3. **Housing** charges may vary depending upon where you choose to live; in a dorm, off-campus in an apartment, or at home, in your old room.
4. **Meal** charges can also vary. There is one figure if purchase a school meal plan. There is another figure if you plan to cook for yourself (usual translation: pasta, pizza, tunafish, and fast food). And there is still a third figure if you're enjoying home-cooked meals—it makes no difference how much this arrangement might add to your parents' normal costs.

5. **Personal expenses** represent all the money you spend at places other than the college. This includes upkeep of clothing, health insurance, even a small allowance for CDs, pizzas, and an occasional night out. The personal expense category can be very flexible. If you are handicapped, for instance, or have child care bills to shoulder, this item can be set very high.
6. **Transportation**, too, is flexible. It may be based on two or three roundtrips (economy class) between a distant campus and home or it may represent commuting expenses.

Expense budgets are established by the financial aid administrator for the different categories of students who attend a typical college. There may be a separate budget for dependent students living in the dorm, dependent students in an apartment, dependent students who live at home, independent students in each of these categories, and subcategories for single and married independent students. In addition, the financial aid administrator will make special allowances in the budget for the unique problems of the handicapped. To illustrate this variety, note the different budgets established by one college in California.

Single Student, Lives at Home	$11,210
Single Student, Lives in Dorm	$14,590
Single Student, Lives in Own Apartment	$15,210
Married Student, Child Care Expenses	$20,830

Here are some points to ponder about expense budgets:

- Some items in the expense budget, such as room and board when you live at home, may not represent a special outlay for your family.
- By being frugal, your actual expenditures may be less than the college has allowed.
- If some of your college-related expenses do not appear to be accurately reflected in the expense budget, let the financial aid administrator know. Any increase in the expense budget increases your eligibility for financial aid.

You can get excellent estimates of college costs from two handy references: The current editions of the College Board's *The College Cost Book* or the ACT's *College Planning/Search Book*. (See your guidance counselor). Of course, you will want to augment this information by writing directly to colleges and asking for their most current catalogue. Also remember, if the information you're using is for the 1994/95 year, and you aren't starting college until 1995/96, you should add 7 or 8% to the total cost figure to get a better idea of the rate you'll be paying.

To get a quick idea of the relationship between your family contribution and college costs, we have developed a cost-of-attendance table for different types of institutions, projected to 1998/99. Despite this year's 10% hike at many public schools (compared to 6% at the privates), we've used a more historical average of 7%. Note that in a four-year, private college, your last year could, conceivably, cost $4690 more than your first.

Type of Institution	1995/96		1996/97		1997/98		1998/99	
	Resident	Commuter	Resident	Commuter	Resident	Commuter	Resident	Commuter
4-Year Private	20,430	17,400	21,860	18,620	23,400	19,900	25,030	21,290
2-Year Private	13,900	11,670	14,875	12,485	15,915	13,360	17,030	14,295
4-Year Public	9,800	7,795	10,500	8,340	11,220	8,925	12,005	9,550
2-Year Public	8,240	6,150	8,815	6,580	9,430	7,040	10,090	7,530

QUESTION #3: WHAT'S MY NEED?

Now you have all the materials you need to answer the third question: How much need will I have at each college of my choice? You do that by comparing your Family Contribution, as determined from Appendix 1, 2, or 3, with the Cost of Attendance (all six elements) at each school that interests you. Remember: If you're applying to one of the wealthier private schools you should perform this comparison twice: once using the federal methodology to determine your eligibility for federal aid, and again using the institutional methodology to determine your eligibility for institutional aid.

EXECUTE THE APPLICATION PROCESS WITH SPEED AND PRECISION

Now that the first element in taking charge has been accomplished (Knowing the Money Numbers Ahead of Time), you can initiate the second element: Executing the Mechanics of the Application Process With Speed and Precision.

You submit your financial aid application form as soon after the first of the year as possible. We say "as soon after" because a great many programs unlocked by the form are time-sensitive. They operate on a first-come, first-served basis.

Table of Agencies, Forms and Programs

Form	Sponsor	Purpose	
		First-Come, First-Served Programs	Programs Not Time Sensitive
Free Application for Federal Student Aid (FAFSA) Renewal FAFSA	Uncle Sam College Scholarship Service (CSS) American College Testing Service (ACT) Pennsylvania Higher Education Assistance Agency (PHEAA)	Federal Campus-Based Programs Most State Programs Some College Programs Some Private Programs	Federal Pell Grant Federal Family Education Loans (Stafford and PLUS) Federal Direct Loans (Direct Stafford, Direct PLUS)
Financial Aid Form (FAF)	College Scholarship Service (CSS)	Some College Programs Some State Programs Some Private Programs	Some College Programs Some State Programs Some Private Programs

Which form should you fill out? That's up to the colleges and your home state. Be sure to find out before January 1. Here are some general guidelines: Everyone must file the Free Application for Federal Student Aid (FAFSA) to be considered for federal student assistance. In addition, some families will have to file the College Board's Financial Aid Form (FAF) or a supplemental form from their home state to be considered for state and collegiate resources. Finally, some families will have to complete an institutional aid form and send it directly to the college they hope to attend. In other words, you may have to file one, two or three forms depending on the wishes of schools to which you apply. Why so many forms? Simple. College is expensive and there's not enough financial aid for everyone, so schools have to figure out who needs money the most. When Congress reauthorized the Higher Education Act, it removed "home equity" from the need analysis calculation. Suddenly zillions more people (mostly middle class people) became eligible for financial aid. Unfortunately, Congress did not appropriate more money to cover its largess so aid administratorshad to tell families, "Sorry, I know you qualify for aid, but we don't have any money to give you." Their solution: (1) Award federal aid to all who qualify; (2) find out more about a family's finances, especially the amount of equity they have in their home, and the income and assets of non custodial parents (if the parents are divorced); (3) adjust the family contribution accordingly; (4) award the limited collegiate (and state) resources to the neediest of the needy; and (5) suggest politely that everyone else borrow more money.

Students applying to in-state schools will frequently get by with filing just the FAFSA. Students applying to more expensive schools...schools where federal and state aid doesn't cover the tuition bill (e.g., private schools and out-of-state public schools)...will usually have to complete the trio of forms, as described above.

The Table of Agencies, Forms and Programs (previous page) lists the most widely used aid applications and the programs they serve (including which are first-come, first served). Where do you get the forms? The FAFSA and FAF come from your guidance office or any college financial aid office. The Renewal FAFSA will come in the mail by January 1 to those students who filed FAFSAs last year..

THE RENEWAL FAFSA

Beginning mid-November, each FAFSA processor will mail renewal applications to students who used that processor during the 1994/95 award year. Renewal FAFSAs will come pre-printed with much of the data you provided last year, so unless there's a change in information, you can skip over many of the questions. If you are using the renewal application be certain to check the names (and codes) of the colleges and state agencies that are to receive the results of your needs analysis. Uncle Sam noted that last year many students neglected to do this, then wondered why the financial aid office never got a copy of their Student Aid Report.

HERE ARE SOME IMPORTANT POINTS

- **Name, Rank and Serial Number.** You must have a social security number to apply for financial aid. Furthermore, the Department of Education now verifies every applicant's name, social security and date of birth with the Social Security Administration. To minimize problems, avoid using nicknames. The computer doesn't know whether "Bill Reese" and "William Reese, Jr." are the same person. Married or divorced students must be especially careful as their last names may have changed, while their social security numbers have not. .
- **January 1.** Financial aid forms cannot be dated or submitted before January 1.
- **Date Due.** Be sure you know when colleges want you to submit the forms. If you apply to six colleges and each has a different date, make a list of these dates, and submit the form by the earliest of the dates on your list. The form, incidentally, goes to the colleges via the need analysis processor, so allow plenty of time.
- **Use the Right Forms.** In trying to simplify the aid process by standardizing the application, Uncle has made things more complex for some students. Read each school's financial aid literature closely to make sure you know which forms to file.
- **Identify Your College Completely.** 8,200 schools participate in Uncle Sam's student aid programs. If Uncle included an institutional code list with each FAFSA packet, he would have no money left to fund aid programs, so it's your responsibility to list schools correctly—this means you must record the full name and complete address of every school that should receive your financial aid information. Remember "U. of M." could mean Maryland or Michigan. "University of California" could mean the campus at Davis or Irvine.
- **Estimating Information.** If the earliest filing date falls before your mom and dad have done their income taxes, you can use income and tax estimates on the FAFSA. If you note, later on, that your estimates were incorrect, you'll have to provide corrections to the processor.
- **Comparison Between Need Analysis Forms and IRS Forms.** College financial aid administrators must verify 30% of all financial aid forms, which means comparing data with that found on your income tax return. This enormous amount of paperwork can delay the distribution of money to students. It also means that if you estimated the information, and were outside a tolerance range, and did not provide any corrections, the college will know and you will be asked to make corrections. Uncle Sam will pick over one million applications for verification, so

accept the fact that tax returns and financial aid forms must match rather closely, and be consistent. Items on the FAFSA which must match with your 1040 include adjusted gross income, income tax paid and number of exemptions. Note: Some schools ask all their students for copies of their tax returns — as a matter of policy.

- **A Good Use of the Winter Holiday.** On a quiet day, switch off the TV, sit down with your family, an income tax form and a financial aid application, and put red circles around the common items. At that time, you may wish to complete an estimated tax return so you can get a headstart on filling out the financial aid form.
- **Be Consistent.** The FAFSA processor is programmed to crosscheck data and flag questionable applications for verification. *Example One*: A dependent student claims a one-parent family but records income for two parents. *Example Two*: A family shows $100,000 in savings, but no unearned income. Conversely, a family shows $10,000 in unearned income, but has no assets. There should be some correlation between the value of your savings and investments and the amount of your unearned income. Otherwise, lights will flash, bells will sound, and investment advice will come pouring in (or, you'll be asked to share your investment secrets). In either case, you're a candidate for verification.
- **College Financial Aid Forms.** Many colleges will ask you to submit their own forms in addition to the major aid forms discussed earlier. These, thank the Heavens, are usually much simpler to fill out.
- **Change in Status.** If, after you have submitted your FAFSA, there is a change in your status (a family death, disability, prolonged unemployment, divorce or separation), notify the college immediately. Financial aid administrators cannot make direct changes to your EFC, however, they can adjust individual data elements (e.g., lower your reportable income or assets) to reflect your new situation.
- **Early Bird Gets the Worm.** Apply for financial assistance as early as possible. Schools can often meet the needs of the first applicants, and then run out of assistance money for the late applicants. The following extract from a letter originating in a college's financial aid office is typical:

  "...The University of X has not been able to meet the financial needs of all students in 1995/96. We are likely to be in this position again during the 1996/97 academic year and late financial aid applicants are likely to be affected."

- **Don't Make Mistakes** when filling out your financial aid applications. Mistakes cause the form to bounce. By the time you make corrections and resubmit it, you will find yourself at the end of the line and the money gone. Most common mistakes: Omitting social security number, recording an incorrect social security number, forgetting to sign the form, leaving questions blank when you really mean zero, (write "0"), using "white-out," entering a range of figures such as $200-400, giving monthly amounts instead of yearly amounts or vice versa (read the question carefully to learn what information is required), entering cents, leaving off numbers ($5,000 vs. $50,000), writing illegibly, and writing in the margins.
- **Don't Falsify Anything.** As the top of the FAFSA clearly states, "If you purposely give false or misleading information on this form, you may be fined $10,000, sent to prison sentence or both." And don't expect the financial planner you hired to bail you out.
- **Make Copies** of all financial aid forms and your responses to requests for added information that may come to you from Uncle Sam, the need analysis processor or the colleges. Make sure to send the original, however, and keep the copy for yourself.
- **If You are Male, Register for Selective Service.** You will not be eligible for financial aid unless you do. If you are exempt from registering for the draft, you must file a statement accordingly.

- **If necessary, include the processing fee.** The FAFSA is free, but the FAF costs $13.75 for the first report and $9.75 for each additional! (This cost is a big reason to make sure you don't waste your time on the FAF unless your college asks you to!)
- **Finally, if you have suggestions on ways to improve and refine the FAFSA for 1996/97, write them down and send them to Uncle Sam.** Every fall, an "Invitation to Comment" appears in the Federal Register. Comments about the form's design and clarity of instructions must be received by the Department of Education (Applicant Systems Division) by mid-December.

WHAT HAPPENS NOW?

Your financial aid application is sent to the need analysis service. The service checks the information. If there is something wrong, the service will contact you. If there is nothing wrong, the service will send your information to a central processor which will then convert your information into an Expected Family Contribution (EFC). The service can also determine your eligibility for a state grant. A summary of all these results is sent to you. Review it carefully to make certain your EFC was calculated using the accurate information. A more detailed analysis is sent to the colleges you named.

The financial aid administrator (FAA) now rolls up the ol' sleeves and goes to work. First, the FAA determines your cost of attendance (or student expense budget). Second, the FAA reviews your expected family contribution . Third, the FAA determines your need (and eligibility for most federal programs). Fourth, the FAA determines your eligibility for collegiate awards—about 35% of all FAAs will adjust the contribution based on policies of their office. And finally, the FAA builds your Financial Aid Package.

THE FINANCIAL AID PACKAGE

The federal Pell Grant is the first layer of every financial aid package (see Chapter 10—only students with EFCs under $2,100 are eligible for Pells).

Next, the financial aid administrator gleefully incorporates any outside scholarships you may have found (that's money the school need not worry about providing you).

Third, if the family still has financial need (in other words, if the cost of college exceeds the amount of your Pell Grant plus your outside scholarships plus your EFC) then the FAA draws on four other federal programs: the Stafford Loan, the Perkins Loan, the Supplemental Educational Opportunity Grant, and College Work-Study. For more information on these federal programs, see Chapter 10.

Fourth, the aid administrator takes another look at your financial need. If the cost of college is still greater than all of your resources (your EFC plus money from all the aid programs just mentioned), the FAA can do one of three things: (1) give you a huge award from the college's own resources; (2) use the Institutional Methodology to adjust your family contribution, and if you still have need, then give you funds from the college's own resources; or (3) apologize for not being able to meet your financial need fully. The college's own resources include special loan programs, unrestricted scholarships or restricted scholarships for which you may qualify. The richer the college, the more resources it will have for this layer in the package.

When awarding money from programs they administer but do not fund (i.e., some of the federal programs), colleges tend to give priority to the neediest of the able. When awarding money from their own funds, colleges tend to give priority to the ablest of the needy.

Finally, the financial aid administrator will approve a PLUS loan. The size of your loan is limited to the total program cost less any financial aid you may have received. In other words, if school costs $10,000 and you receive $5,000 in financial aid, you may receive a PLUS loan of $5,000. The size of your family contribution does not matter so long as your parents are credit worthy. For more on PLUS loans, see Chapter 10.

THE AWARD LETTER

The financial aid package will be presented to you in the form of an award letter. The award letter should contain three substantive and two administrative elements.

The substantive elements are (1) a statement of the expense budget developed for you; (2) your family contribution; and (3) the amount of your need, to include how all or part of that need is to be met, listing each aid source and dollar amount.

The administrative elements contain (1) a suspense date by which you must return the award letter and (2) information on available procedures for "appealing" any information in the award letter with which you disagree.

Compare the award letters you receive from all the colleges to which you applied. But don't delay responding to an award letter because you are still waiting for letters from other colleges. If you don't reply by the required date, your award will be cancelled (colleges can't hold money). Responding to the award letter does not commit you to attendance. It just safeguards your award, should you elect to go to that college. In responding to the award letter, you can accept the award in its entirety, accept some components of the award and reject others, reject the award entirely, or request a revision in the composition of awards (more grants, less loans).

Your success in appealing an award depends on a great number of factors; your timing, whether the college has any discretionary funds, how badly the college wants you, how skillful and diplomatic you are in presenting your case, changes in your family situation of which the financial aid administrator was unaware, etc. You should not enter this phase of the financial aid process without first reading our publication *Financial Aid Officers: What They Do — To You and For You* (see inside back cover).

WILL THE NEED-BASED ROUTE SATISFY MY NEED?

Maybe. Maybe not. If it does, it could be a dream package. But, it could also be an offer that leaves you a thousand dollars short or mires you deeply in debt. Remember:
- The fact that you have need does not necessarily mean your family's income qualifies for all assistance programs. Many programs have income ceilings.
- The college may not have enough resources to help all applicants.
- Different colleges may assess your need differently. If you apply to three schools, each of which costs $3,000 more than your family's EFC, you may be offered three very different packages, ranging from the attractive to the unacceptable.

KNOWING WHERE THE INFLUENCE POINTS ARE

Now that you've mastered the mechanics of need analysis, it's time for the third element of the take-charge process: Knowing where the influence points are.

Influence Point: Wise college selection
What You Can Gain: Improved financial aid package; no-need scholarships
More Information: Chapter 9

Influence Point: Careful preparation for need-analysis
What You Can Gain: A lowered family contribution and increased eligibility for aid; Longer planning time for help with cash-flow requirements
More Information: This chapter, Chapter 7, Appendices 1, 2 and 3

Influence Point: Speed and accuracy in applying
What You Can Gain: Increased chance of tapping into limited aid sources; Improved financial aid package.
More Information: This chapter

Influence Point: Working with financial aid administrators
What You Can Gain: Improved financial aid package.
More Information: This chapter, Chapter 7, Chapter 9

A Final Word to the Wise. There is more money in being an informed consumer and taking charge of the aid link-up process than in all the scholarship hunts ever conducted!

Part III
Advanced Moves in Financial Aid

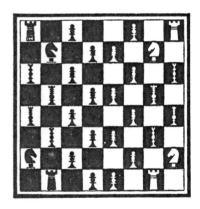

Chapter 7
For the Short Range:
Tilting Things Your Way

NO-NEED AWARDS

No-need awards are scholarships given with no regard to your financial need. If you win a $2,000, no-need academic scholarship, you are $2,000 ahead.

The recipient of a no-need scholarship can fall into one of two categories with regard to college costs: 1. Has need; 2. Doesn't have need. Let's examine each situation in more detail:

Situation 1 — You have need and receive a no-need award. The cost of college is then reduced by the amount of your award. This reduction may eliminate (1) part of your need; (2) your entire need; or (3) your entire need and part of your family contribution. In either case, colleges are required (by federal regulation) to include the award as part of your family's expected resources for college.

Actual numbers will determine which of these it will be. Assume the cost of college is $8,000 and your family contribution is $5,000. This makes your need $3,000. Example 1 — Your no-need award is $1,000. Offered aid package: Your need is reduced from $3,000 to $2,000; your family contribution remains at $5,000. Example 2 — Your no-need award is $3,000. Offered aid package: Your need is wiped out; your family contribution remains $5,000. Example 3 — Your no-need award is $4,000. Offered aid package: Your need is wiped out; this time your family contribution is reduced from $5,000 to $4,000.

Situation 2 — You have no need and the award is a no-need award. In this case, the money goes directly to you. It replaces your money. You write a smaller check when you pay the college bill. Let's assign numbers to this. Your family contribution is $8,000 and the cost of college is $8,000; Example 1 — Your no-need award is $3,000. Your family contribution shrinks to $5,000. That's all you have to pay. Example 2 — Your no-need award is $10,000. You are now $2,000 ahead which will finance your winter vacation on the Amalfi Coast. Right? Wrong. You can only receive $8,000 — the amount that eliminates your family contribution. Tuition aid of any kind, need based or not, cannot exceed the cost of attendance. Financial aid, in other words, cannot produce income for you.

Question. These no-need awards sound great. Where can I find one?

Answer. They tend to congregate in the following three areas.

Uncle Sam. The Federal government has two types of no-need awards. The first is for outstanding students as defined by each individual state (for example, The Robert C. Byrd Honors Scholarship Program — See Chapter 10). The second has a military connection and carries a service obligation. Good examples: the service academies, ROTC scholarships. See Chapter 13.

The States. Two types of programs. One — honor scholarships for outstanding students. Two — tuition equalization grants for in-state students who attend a private college rather than a public university. Both programs usually require students to remain in their home state. See Chapter 11 to learn whether your state operates either program.

The Colleges. Colleges are the main source of no-need awards. Most are academic scholarships designed to entice bright students to enroll at the sponsoring institution. See Chapter 9, 18, and *The A's and B's of Academic Scholarships* (see inside back cover).

LESSONS FROM THE APPENDICES

We assume that while reading Chapter 6 you took the time to complete the worksheets in Appendix 1, 2, or 3 to estimate your family contribution. These are the items that should have caught your eye.

1. **Asset Assessment Rates.** A dependent student does not rate an asset protection allowance. The dependent student's assets are taxed at 35% of their value. Parents do rate an asset protection allowance. Money held by parents, as you trace it through the formula, is taxed about 5.6%. That's quite a difference! $35,000 in junior's bank account becomes a $12,250 contribution to college costs. The same $35,000 in the parental account becomes a mere $1,960 contribution. Lesson: Accumulate money for college, yes. But don't be so quick to accumulate in the child's name.

2. **The True Value of a Student Aid Dollar.** If you are in a 28% tax bracket and don't get student aid, you must earn $1.39 to have one dollar available for tuition bills. Let's turn this around. If you are successful in getting one dollar of student aid, that one dollar is really worth $1.39 to you. Lesson: The higher your tax bracket, the greater the value of any student aid dollar received.

3. **The Previous Year Rule.** Your 1994 earnings determine your aid eligibility for the 1995/96 academic year. Your 1995 earnings impact on the 1996/97 school year. If your income fluctuates, and you have some control over the fluctuations, you might wish to defer income from the base year to the next. That would enhance your eligibility in the coming academic year. What about the next base year? Life is filled with soap opera twists. Take it one year at a time.

4. **Federal Income Tax Versus Student Aid Eligibility.** Federal income taxes have a distinct relationship to student aid eligibility. Pay more in taxes and your aid eligibility increases; pay less in taxes and your aid eligibility decreases. You may want to keep this relationship in mind before you engage in tax reduction schemes such as buying into a tax shelter or making a large donation to a charity. For a family whose adjusted available income (Line 21 in Appendix 1) is over $20,100 per year, each additional tax dollar paid will increase aid eligibility by $0.47; each tax dollar saved will reduce aid eligibility by $0.47.

Question. Why are you telling me all this? How can I take advantage of this knowledge?

Answer. It's all in the numbers. Suppose that by working the appendices you determine you will have $450 of need at College A, your first choice school. A $450 need may qualify you for a Stafford Loan but finding a lender for a loan under $500 will be very difficult. Now, through an accounting maneuver, you manage to increase your federal taxes by $110. What happens? Your need will grow from $450 to $501. A need of over $500 makes finding a lender easy. That is $501 your parents won't have to cover with a check. Even after paying $110 more in taxes, their checking balance will be $391 ahead.

5. **Business Property.** Assets held by an individual are taxed on a dollar for dollar basis. Assets that are part of a business rate an adjustment factor (e.g., 40% of net worth up to $80,000). Think hard. Do you have any source of income, from a hobby or property or whatever, that you can treat as a business? Or can you shift assets to a sub-S corporation in which your family holds a controlling 51% interest while people outside the need analysis formula (your grandmother?) hold 49%? That's a real one-two punch. Not only do you get the asset value reduced by the net worth adjustment, but there is a second reduction stemming from the 49% value transfer outside the immediate family. All this will make your tax return more complex, but the trade-off is a sharply reduced contribution to college costs.

6. **Consumer Debt.** Under need analysis, you get no credit for consumer debt. If you owe the bank $15,000 in car payments, that's your problem. But let's say you own stocks and have a brokerage account that lets you borrow against your portfolio.

If you draw $15,000 from this account to buy the new car, you have in effect reduced the value of your reportable assets by that amount. You pay less for college and have a new car to boot!

TILTING THINGS YOUR WAY

There are five strategies available for tilting the financial aid process in your favor. Only two of the strategies are mutually exclusive. The Napoleon of aid seekers would probably investigate all five.

STRATEGY 1—REDUCING THE FAMILY CONTRIBUTION

Objective: Reduce your family contribution so that your need becomes larger. In other words, make yourself eligible for more student assistance. We offer this advice with the hope you'll be able to distinguish between working with the system and cheating it. There's a fine line between using information about financial aid rules to make certain you get your fair share, and abusing information about financial aid rules at the direct expense of needier students. Keep in mind that many financial aid offices are working with a fixed (small) amount of aid to distribute, so increasing one student's award is only possible by decreasing another's. Also remember, most aid is "need-based," not "want-based." That said, here are some ideas to ponder.

Methods:

1. **Thoroughly understand the need analysis process,** the factors considered, the percentages and weights assigned to the data. Determine whether you can make adjustments in your situation so that you will be treated in a way that is more advantageous to you.

2. **Reduce the value of assets you report for need analysis (I).** Under "Lessons From the Appendices" we talked about why parental assets count less than student assets. We talked about how certain loans can be used to reduce assets. And we talked about the possibilities of shifting assets to "sole proprietorships" or corporations. But there is more.

3. **Reduce the value of your assets (II).** Home equity is not a reportable asset under the Federal Methodology. So what happens if you use some of your savings to pay down your home mortgage? You'll probably be in a much better position to qualify for a low-interest federal loan! Please note, however, financial aid administrators are still free to ask questions about home equity, and may reserve the school's own funds for renters (and expect families with pricey homes and no mortgage to borrow against this great asset).

4. **Reduce the value of your assets (III).** Do you need to make a large purchase before you sign and date your need analysis form? We've already suggested purchasing a car. How about a new stereo, refrigerator or washer-dryer? Pay cash for the purchase, if you can. That will substantially reduce your reportable assets—and provide you with good music, some cold drinks and a few clean clothes.

5. **Use the student's assets first.** If you have been saving money in your child's name, get his or her permission to use that money to pay your entire family contribution for the first year of college. (You could also use the money for something smaller, like the increasingly essential personal computer). This will improve your chances for aid during years two, three, and four. Warning: This won't work at all schools. One of the Ivy's, for example, expects 35% of a student's assets in Year One, 35% of the remaining balance in Year Two, etc. Tricky, tricky, tricky!

6. **Declare yourself independent.** Independent students do not include their parents' income and assets in their need analysis calculation; only their own, (generally) more limited resources. Hence, their contribution will usually be smaller, and their need larger.

   Should you declare yourself independent then, to gain access to more aid? Certainly, if you are really independent and can convince the financial aid administrator accordingly. Absolutely not, if it is a ploy. Please note: The definition of "independent" was tightened during the 1993/94 school year. Single, undergraduate students under the age of 24 are considered "dependent" in all cases, except at the discretion of the financial aid administrator.

7. **Use the most favorable need analysis method.** Families with adjusted gross incomes under $50,000 who are eligible to file a 1040A or 1040EZ (even if they actually file a regular 1040) may use the Simplified Methodology to calculate family contribution. In other words, neither parent nor student assets are considered for need analysis. If you are eligible to file a 1040A or 1040EZ and can keep your AGI under $50,000, do so!

8. **Take less pay.** Is there any way for you to defer year-end bonuses? Remember, need analysis looks at previous year income — 1994 for the 1995/96 award year. As Uncle Sam monitors the impact of the Higher Education Amendments on the federal budget and on middle income families, who knows what adjustments he'll make in program regulations. With constantly changing rules, if you can increase your eligibility even for a year, do it!

9. **Accelerate or postpone gains and losses.** If you plan to sell stocks or property, do it two years before college, or wait until your student has graduated. Realized gains count as income which is heavily "taxed" by the need analysis system.

10. **Start a family business.** It doesn't have to be complex. Some examples. The Bakers started Babycakes, Inc. to sell muffins every Saturday morning at their local farmer's market. Rose loved going to yard sales on weekends, so, she started a second hand furniture business with the objects she found. Phil loved to buy the "mystery boxes" of stamps advertised in auction catalogues. He and his daughter would wash and sort the stamps, then resell them to other collectors. Uncle Sam rewards private enterprise with a greatly reduced expected contribution to college costs. Also remember, any money you pay your children becomes a business expense, and under the Federal Methodology, students receive an income protection allowance of $1,750.

11. **Save for retirement.** Need analysis wants to know how much you contribute to a retirement fund the year before college (it considers this contribution a discretionary item and adds it back in to your total income). It does not, however, ask how much you've already saved. In other words, you can accumulate money tax-free (or tax-deferred) at the same time you reduce your assets for need analysis and save for your retirement. Please note, however, that some colleges will ask about the value of your retirement funds and ask you to borrow against them. Also, you don't want all your assets tied up in funds that penalize you for early withdrawal (e.g., before age 59 1/2). You may need some money sooner.

12. **Extraordinary Expenses.** Does your family have enormous medical expenses? Does your family pay private secondary school tuitions for younger siblings? Were your parents divorced or separated after you filed your aid application? Was your home affected by the California earthquakes or the Midwest floods? The Federal Methodology no longer includes allowances for unreimbursed medical expenses, secondary tuition paid, or unpleasant events like the ones just mentioned, but leaves consideration of these special conditions to the discretion of the financial aid administrator. Make certain to let the FAA know!

13. **Go complex.** If you choose this option, be willing to pay a personal financial planner — one who really understands student aid (and such planners are not easy to find). Here is a gem from Marty Singer, CFP, a partner at Summit Financial Resources (4 Campus Drive, Parsippany, New Jersey 07054, 201/285-3679).

"...The two key methods of increasing aid eligibility are to reduce Adjusted Gross Income and to move assets outside the view of the financial aid formulas. Employees of large companies have little chance to reduce formula income. If, however, you work for a small corporation, or if you are self-employed, you may be able to arrange a deferred compensation agreement where the employer reduces your salary in return for larger payments after the children are educated.

Small business owners have great control over their reported earnings and can postpone income by reinvesting profits in business equipment, setting up a pension plan or creating their own deferred compensation program. Since the aid formulas favor business assets with a substantial protection allowance, it is advantageous to convert money that would otherwise be income into a business asset.

"For most middle-income families, the greatest opportunity to qualify for more financial aid comes from repositioning assets, by moving them outside the view of the formula. One way to do this is to mortgage your house to the hilt. Take the proceeds, most of your savings, and all of your child's money and redeploy them in tax-deferred investment vehicles. For example, nowhere does the FAFSA ask for the cash value of life insurance or deferred annuities. Your money will be safe and earn tax-deferred interest.

"Although home equity is now excluded from the formula which determines eligibility for government grants and loans, financial aid administrators will likely find this asset hard to overlook when awarding aid from the college's own funds. How can they ask the same payment from Kimberly's family which owns no home as they do of Jennifer's parents who have a $175,000 house with only a $20,000 remaining mortgage?

"All else equal, I think Kim will get a college grant and Jennifer will be given a roadmap to the nearest bank offering home equity loans.

"Even if financial aid were not an issue, it often makes sense to borrow at today's low interest rates and invest the proceeds in tax deferred mutual funds so long as the investment fits in with the family's overall financial plan.

"Of course, a careful cash flow analysis is essential. You will now have sizeable monthly mortgage payments in addition to your (reduced) contribution to college costs. But, by using a properly-structured universal life policy, you can keep your money out of the formula yet still have it readily available. Within limits, you may make tax-free withdrawals without penalty to provide yourself adequate cash flow to meet all your obligations. Amounts not needed during the college years may be invested in fixed or variable annuities to provide tax-deferred growth, investment balance and diversification.

"If the plan is set up properly, you may find yourself with greatly increased financial aid, considerable income tax savings, a diversified investment program, and inexpensive life insurance paid for with untaxed dollars all at the same time. Warning: The value and features of insurance policies and contracts vary widely, and there are many complicated rules that must be followed to protect the tax-free status of insurance withdrawals.

"Strategies like the one just described have made it possible for parents to provide their children with the best education for which they qualify without breaking the family piggy bank. But you should not attempt to set up such a plan yourself. You will need to consult a knowledgeable professional to guide you through the many traps that await the inexperienced adventurer."

STRATEGY 2—INCREASING THE COST OF ATTENDANCE

Objective: Increase the cost of attendance so your need becomes larger. This technique is especially appropriate for improving your chances for a Stafford Loan.

Methods:

1. **Pick a more expensive school** if you assume there is a direct relationship between cost and quality of education. Example: Your family contribution is $5,000 and you plan to attend a $6,000 school. The maximum (subsidized) Stafford Loan for which you qualify is $1,000. If you now select a $7,500 school, you could qualify for a $2,500 loan. Remember, your family contribution does not change.

2. **Be sure all your expenses are reflected in the "Cost of Attendance."** Does the financial aid administrator have a true picture of your transportation costs, special medical expenses, or other legitimate expenses that may have been overlooked by the school? Unfortunately, FAAs cannot include the cost of a new computer in your cost of attendance figure UNLESS the school explicitly requires all students to own one (many do)! Here, however, is a situation that can work! Your family contribution is $5,000 and the financial aid administrator has established a $6,000 cost of attendance for you. The maximum (subsidized) Stafford Loan for which you can qualify is $1,000. You now convince the financial aid administrator your budget must include $500 for physical therapy made necessary by a recent car accident. Your budget now becomes $6,500 and you qualify for a $1,500 Stafford Loan.

Now you try one. Unbeknownst to the financial aid administrator (as well as the admission committee), one incoming student is a werewolf. What will be the student's extra expenses? Bars for the windows. Dead bolt locks. Paying for roomie to stay at the Holiday Inn during every full moon. An occasional sack of Purina dog chow. Flea collars. Rabies shots. City dog tags. A monthly shampoo and pedicure. You complete the list...

STRATEGY 3—OBTAINING AN IMPROVED AID PACKAGE

The aid package that covers your need is loaded with loan money that, one day, you will have to repay. You don't like that.

Objective: Change the composition of the aid package to emphasize assistance that does not have to be repaid—grants and work-study opportunities.

Methods:

1. **Apply to colleges as early as possible,** before their money runs out.
2. **Pick a college where you are in the top 25% of the applicant pool.** The most desirable applicants get the most agreeable aid packages. That's as true at the Ivies as it is at Horned Toad State.
3. **If necessary, negotiate with the financial aid administrator.** But remember, you can negotiate only if the college really wants you. What gives you bargaining strength? Good grades and high SATs, athletic ability, artistic talents, alumni ties, ethnic background, geographic origin, even a substantial financial aid package from one of the school's "competitors." Colleges like to brag the diversity of their student body and they might be missing a pole vaulter from Idaho or a soprano from Rhode Island. Colleges also know they are competing for warm bodies. You might even ask a department head (if you are a genius) or a coach (if you are a triple-threat) to be your ally and advocate in such negotiations. Why do colleges care so much about all this? Long term survival! First of all, a diverse student body does in fact make for a more rewarding academic experience for all enrolled students, but also, having an enthusiastic, diverse group of alumni spread out over the country is a good way for a college to ensure a continued stream of applicants in future years.
4. **Find Scholarships.** Locate outside scholarships. These scholarships can improve your aid package if part of their value is used to replace a loan element (that decision rests with the FAA).

STRATEGY 4—REPLACING YOUR MONEY WITH OPM (OTHER PEOPLE'S MONEY)

Objective: Getting somebody else's money to pay for your expected family contribution is the most desirable but also the most difficult strategy. People often think that by finding a scholarship—any scholarship—they have replaced their own contribution. That, of course, is not so. The scholarship usually just becomes part of your family's expected resources.

Method: Qualify for a "no-need" scholarship. See opening section of this chapter.

Attempt to lower the cost of college so as to reduce or eliminate your need.

Objective: To avoid going through the hassle of applying for aid or saddling yourself with debt following graduation.

Methods:

1. **Pick a lower-priced school** such as one in an area where the cost of living is low (e.g., Texas, Michigan) or one that receives church subsidies (e.g., Brigham Young, St. Olaf). And most importantly, don't overlook your own State U.

2. **Examine each of the six elements that make up "cost of attendance"** at a college. Some are firmly established (such as tuition), but others can be influenced. For example, used books cost less than new ones and many airlines have incredible student rates! (or you might consider paying tuition with an airline's credit card and use the resulting frequent flier miles for free round trips to campus).

3. **Accelerate college** by taking college courses for credit while in high school or by getting credit on advanced placement exams. About 1,200 schools give credit for good AP scores; hundreds (including Harvard) even grant incoming students sophomore standing. Each credit hour you pick up can be worth as much as $300 (depending on the college's tuition costs).

   Another option is the three-year degree. High profile figures from Stanford and Oberlin have praised the idea. (Others feel most students really need the full four years to grow, intellectually, emotionally, and occupationally. They're afraid the liberal-arts will get short-changed as students won't have enough time to take the necessary spectrum of courses). Middlebury College and Valparaiso University are launching trial three-year programs this fall. Albertus Magnus College introduced its tri-session plan last year (if students attend three 13-week sessions per year instead of two 15-week sessions they can graduate in three years and save $20,000).

4. **Go to a community college for two years,** then transfer to a four-year school to finish your degree. You pick up the "halo" of the prestige college's sheepskin, but at a fraction of the cost.

5. **Investigate external degree programs.** Take correspondence courses, or study at home. Regents College seems the most comprehensive. For course and program information, write Regents College Degrees, Cultural Education Center, Albany, NY, 12230.

   Another option worth investigating is education through public television. Many stations have agreements with colleges to offer courses for credit. Mind Extension University, in conjunction with Colorado State University (and others), lets cable subscribers get course credit at home, that may later be applied toward degree programs at most colleges. Sample courses include: Analytical Geometry and Calculus, American Poetry Post-1900, Family Relationships, Conversational French, the US Constitution, and Economics (Macro- and Micro-). Call 800-777-MIND for tuition and registration information. An even larger program (more than 300,000 tuition-paying viewers per year via 2,000 affiliated colleges) is the Public Broadcasting System's Adult Learning Service. *Warning*: Make sure you check the accreditation for all of these programs. Nonaccredited courses will not count toward a degree. Also. Don't try to argue that a $4,000 wide screen TV should be part of your cost of college figure! This strategy won't get you far in your quest for student aid.

   Our guess is that computers, modems and phone lines will be the next wave in external degree programs. The aptly named Thomas Edison State College (Trenton, NJ), for example, with its 9,000 students, has no faculty, no library, no student center, and no football team. In fact its hub is little more than a 2 foot by 3 foot Digital Equipment Corporation VAX 4000 computer. The school contracts with 300 faculty members at nearby schools to "supervise" courses. Accepted students receive a course package that includes textbooks and videos and software for phone connections. They use electronic mail to communicate with faculty (called mentors) and other classmates, get reading assignments, and submit papers. Classroom "discussions" (via E-mail) are extensive. Only graduation still takes place on campus!

6. **Get credit for life experience.** Different schools have their own rules on what experiences count for what credit. The American Council on Education publishes guidelines in a book called The National Guide to Educational Credit for Training Programs. Another option is to take the College Board's College-Level Examination Program (CLEP) Test.

The best summary of external degree programs is a book by John Bear published by Ten Speed Press, PO Box 7123, Berkeley, CA 94707.

HELP WITH THE CASH FLOW

Your family contribution must be paid each semester. For those who have assembled vast quantities of worldly goods, the family contribution can represent a rather sizable sum that usually comes with a friendly note "unless this bill is paid by such and such a date your student will not be allowed to register for classes..."

How can you pay this bill without selling the family home, jeopardizing your after-retirement financial security or taking out a high-cost commercial loan? You could turn to Uncle Sam's Federal Family Education Loan Program (the Stafford and PLUS—see Chapter 10). But Uncle's loans have some drawbacks. One, payments on the PLUS start within 60 days of taking out the loan. Two, they are subject to the whims of the political process. And, three, they have the usual comet's tail of paperwork, back-and-forth mailings, and other rigmarole generally attached to federal programs.

Objective: To pay your family contribution without liquidating assets, hocking the family jewels, or playing Uncle Sam's paper games.

Methods:

1. **Select a college that offers favorable, middle-income loan programs,** either from its own endowment funds or through money raised by state tax-exempt bond issues (more on these in Chapter 9).
2. **Select a college that permits you to pay the family contribution in installments** (Chapter 9).
3. **Participate in a commercial college tuition payment plan.** Here is how some plans work: You predetermine your cash requirement for college—say $3,000 at the start of each semester. The commercial organization collects ($250) monthly payments from you and forwards that money to the school (based on schedules established by the school). Your payments are deferred and spread evenly over a number of months (you pay no interest, but usually have to start making payments before your account is due). Frequently, the plans have a life insurance feature that covers bills in the event of your death or total disability. Sponsors of this, and tuition credit line plans include:

    Knight College Resource Group. 800/225-6783 (or 617/267-1500)

    Tuition Management Systems. 42 Valley Road, Newport, RI 02840, 800/722-4867 (students and parents); 800/356-0350 (administrators) and 401/849-1550 (in Rhode Island).

    Academic Management Services. 50 Vision Blvd., East Providence, RI 02914, 800-635-0120

    Education Credit Corporation, 140 Mayhew Way, Suite 100, Pleasant Hill, CA 94523, 800/477-4977.

    Many of these plans are also a source for commercial loans (see below)
4. **Borrow from a commercial loan source.** But be sure to compare plans before you sign on any dotted lines. Finance charges can vary greatly, as can the repayment schedules. Here are four of the largest lenders/guarantors:

    TERI offers loans of up to the total cost of education with 25 years to repay. Repayment begins 45 days after the college receives the loan money (although

41

families may defer paying back the principal for up to 4 years while the student is enrolled). Other costs consist of a guarantee fee equal to 5% of the total loan amount. The interest rate equals the prime rate plus 1-2%. TERI also sponsors the Professional Education Plan (PEP) for graduate students. Contact The Education Resource Institute, 330 Stuart Street, Suite 500, Boston, MA 02116, 1-800-255-TERI. This plan comes under a variety of other names (for example, VALUE and Alliance) depending on the plan's cosponsor. TERI acts as the guarantor.

NELLIE MAE. The New England Loan Marketing Association offers similar loans (EXCEL. GradEXCEL and SHARE). For more information, write Nellie Mae, 50 Braintree Hill Park, Suite 300, Braintree, MA 02184, 800-634-9308 (in MA, 617-849-3447)

SALLIE MAE. The Student Loan Marketing Association offers a wide variety of programs for both graduate and undergraduate students. In conjunction with the College Board, for example, you can borrow an amount equal to the cost of tuition, room and board, and fees each year at an interest rate equal to the 91-day T-bill plus 4.5%. For more information on the Extra Credit Loan, write SALLIE MAE, 1050 Thomas Jefferson Street, NW, Washington, DC 20007, 800-874-9390

PLATO. Loans of up to $25,000 per year with 15 years to repay. Repayment begins 30 days after the student receives the loan money (although families may defer repaying the principal for up to four years while the student is enrolled). The interest rate equals the previous month's commercial paper note rate plus 4.85%. Contact ConSern, 205 Van Buren St. #200, Herndon, VA 22070, 800-GO-PLATO.

5. **Tap your home equity.** If your family has a good income and credit history, you can generally borrow up to 80% of the market value of your home minus the outstanding balance of your mortgage. In other words, if you own a $100,000 home and have $30,000 remaining on the mortgage, you can borrow up to $50,000. Calculation: (100,000 x .8)-30,000=$50,000. There is a small fee to open the account, but after that, you can borrow whatever amount you need, whenever you need it, without ever having to reapply. To use the funds, you simply write a check or use a credit card. Interest rates float about two percentage points above the prime. And here's an added bonus. Any items you charge against your credit line—like college tuition—will become part of your home mortgage, so, your interest payments on loans up to $100,000 become tax-deductible (unless the proceeds are used to buy annuities or tax-exempt bonds). Home equity loans are an extremely easy and flexible way to obtain cash flow assistance on favorable terms. In fact, they allow many families to live way beyond their means, so care must be taken that ease of access to all this money does not result in deep financial problems and cause you to lose your home. The total monthly payments on all of your loans should not exceed 35% of your pre-tax monthly income.

Here are some questions to ask before you take out a home equity loan: What is the initial rate of interest? If it's variable, how often can the rate change? On what index is it based? Does it carry a cap? Is there an annual fee? An application fee? An origination fee? Can any of the terms be changed without my approval? Are there any points charged? What about closing costs? Under what circumstances can the bank require repayment of the outstanding credit?

6. **Borrow against your 401(k).** If you participate in a company pension or profit-sharing plan like a 401(k), you may be able to borrow against the equity built up in it. Or, if you are a self-employed professional with a retirement plan, you can do some borrowing. Under tax reform, you can borrow half the amount you have vested up to $50,000, less your highest loan balance during the preceding 12 months. The interest rate hovers around the prime, you pay no fees or points, and the cash is available very quickly. To avoid tax and penalties you must repay your account within five years (you have longer if the money is used to buy a home). Payments are usually made via payroll deductions. If you decide to use this option, make certain to borrow enough to cover a full year's tuition, not just a

semester, since employers may impose additional regulations, such as only one loan per year. If at all possible, however, consider borrowing from some other source. Raids on your 401(k) will cause your fund to grow at a much slower pace, and if you're like most parents, you really do need this money for your retirement.

7. **Draw out some of the money accumulated in an IRA account.** You'll probably be hit with a 10% penalty and a bill from the IRS, so, if you need $6,000, draw out a little extra to take care of both the bursar and Uncle Sam. As usual, there is an exception. This time it's found in Section 72(t)(2)(A)(iv) of the tax code (or thereabouts). You can escape the tax collector and withdraw funds before you turn 59 1/2, provided you receive the money in equal, periodic payments extending over the rest of your years. You can even eventually modify these payments — after the later of five years or turning 59 1/2.

"WHAT IF" CALCULATIONS

Every sophisticated family should try a few "what if" situations, using the worksheets in Appendix 1, 2, or 3. If you have a home computer with spreadsheet software, these appendices are easily programmed, and make "what-if" calculations simple. Another option is to order our software package (see inside back cover). The results can surprise you.

Here are a few "what-if" suggestions.

1. How does a charitable gift of $1,000 or $2,000 impact on your family contribution?
2. Should Mom get a job to help with college costs? Or, should Mom quit her job to increase eligibility for financial aid?
3. If Dad needs to complete his degree, is there any advantage to his returning to school at the same time one or more children are in college?
4. If you have two children, one year apart, with one starting college and one starting the senior year in high school, would it be advantageous for the older child to "stop out" for one year and wait for son or daughter #2 to catch up?
5. Do grandparents need some extra money? You can each give each of your student's grandparents a gift of up to $10,000. That could reduce your assets by as much as $80,000. It could also reduce the amount of tax being paid, as frequently, grandparents are retired and in a lower tax bracket.
6. Can you shift some assets into a business venture?
7. Can you lower your AGI to under $50,000?
8. What happens if you make a large purchase, such as a car, and pay cash or borrow against a stock portfolio?
9. What happens if you pay down your mortgage?
10. Try some "what-ifs" of your own.

WHAT PEOPLE WON'T TRY

1. **Students buy campus property.** Linda Wallace, a University of Wisconsin student, purchased a condominium near the campus for $60,000. When she graduated, she sold it for a $30,000 profit — enough to pay off four years of college expenses.

   Becky and Louis James moved to San Diego to attend the University of California. They bought a three-bedroom house, converted a shed into a fourth bedroom, and collected rent from roommates. The James' are tickled pink with their investment. The rent covers mortgage payments. And, by owning property, the James' established California residency, saving each more than $1,000 a year in out-of-state tuition.

   Of course, Linda and the James' also saved on college room and board charges.
2. **Mom and Dad buy campus rental property.** This takes a more sophisticated approach. Not only do you get the benefits of annual deductions for mortgage interest, operating expenses and depreciation, but your college student offspring

can receive a steady salary while in school; a salary you may deduct as a business expense. How? By having that son or daughter live in one of the units and draw pay from you as residential property manager. At the same time, he or she saves on room and board. In addition, your campus visits can be written off, because, as far as the tax collector is concerned, the purpose of the trip is to inspect the condition of your property. And, if your real estate appreciates, you can sell the property and pocket the after tax share of the capital gain. There is still one more advantage. If you purchase the property (or make a down payment on the property) with funds that used to be personal assets, and you make certain the property becomes part of a formally recognized business, you have moved them into the business category which provides you with a net worth adjustment in the need analysis formula.

To take advantage of all this, be sure your property qualifies as rental property (and not personal property). In other words, Mom or Dad cannot use it for more than 14 days or 10% of the total days they rent it out. Here's why: Uncle Sam and the IRS distinguish between the treatment of personal property and the treatment of rental property. The IRS limits deductible losses from the rental of personal property to the amount of rental income received. The IRS places no such limit on losses from rental property, however, these losses may no longer be used to offset salary income. They may only be used to offset what the IRS calls passive income—income from limited partnerships or other rental property. Further-more, the IRS limits the deduction of mortgage interest to the amount allocated to rental use (if, however, the property is rented for 100% of the year, 100% of the mortgage interest may still be deducted). There is still some good news in all this. Families with AGIs under $100,000 who actively manage their property, may use up to $25,000 of real estate losses to shelter "nonpassive" (salary) income. NOTE: The IRS has 266 pages of rules on passive/active losses. We've tried to summarize it in the paragraphs above, but still suggest you speak with an accountant or tax attorney before you undertake this kind of venture.

3. **Get on Mom or Dad's payroll.** Can either of your parents give you a job in the family business? If so, it's a great way to shift some income! Your earnings become a tax deductible business expense. If you're under 18, you do not have to pay social security tax on your wages. And, if you can limit your earnings to under $3,800 per year ($5,800 if you contribute to an IRA), you will owe no federal income tax. Assuming you start this when you enter high school and your parents pay about 40% in federal, state and local taxes, they will receive $9,280 in deductions. Of course, under the federal methodology, schools will grab about $7,345 of the $23,200 you've earned. Calculation: 35% of all non-retirement assets (c. $15,200) plus 50% of prior year income ($5,800) over $1,750, but isn't that what the money was for anyway?. Meanwhile, you're also beginning to save for retirement. Even without additional contributions, your $8,000 IRA (at 8%) will grow to nearly $335,000 by the time you're 65!

4. **Give a gift.** An individual can make a $10,000 tax-free gift each year to another individual. A married couple can double that and make it a $20,000 gift. Under conventional wisdom, grandparents are the ones who usually take advantage of this tax wrinkle to help their smart grandchildren with college. Under unconventional wisdom, (as we explained under "what-ifs" to try) parents might consider making an annual gift to grandparents. The purpose: To reduce their own asset position for need analysis and pay less for college. The money, meanwhile, really did not leave the family. A gift of securities is especially advantageous. If they have appreciated, you avoid paying tax on the gain. And, if they continue to appreciate after they have been transferred, they can be inherited at this higher value, and still no one has had to pay tax on the gain.

6. **Start an educational benefit trust.** Small, closely held corporations can establish trusts to pay the college expenses of employees' children—that means all employ-

ees—the president's as well as the staff's. The corporation makes regular payments to the trust. The trust, which is governed by a bank or attorney not connected with the corporation, then invests the funds which accumulate tax-free. Once an eligible person reaches college age, a predetermined amount of tuition money is withdrawn. This disbursement must be treated as a taxable benefit by the student's parents. Thus, the president who is in a higher bracket will probably gain less than a member of the staff.

7. **Start a company scholarship program.** This is not as complex as a trust. Still, the program must meet an IRS test to qualify as a business expense. The test usually involves a set of standards. For example, beneficiaries must have a B average; their mother or father must have worked for the company at least five years. A second part of the test deals with eligibility. All employees' children must be eligible. If too many scholarships go to the children of corporate officers and directors, the company will flunk the test.

8. **Borrow against a brokerage account.** This is another way to avoid the "nondeductibility of consumer interest" feature of the tax laws. If the loan is used to buy investment property, interest is deductible up to the amount of investment income produced. We suggest you sell some securities to pay your college bills, then use a loan to buy more securities (Note: You can't deduct interest on a loan used to buy tax-exempt investments such as municipal bonds, because you don't pay tax on the resulting income from these bonds). If you do decide to borrow against your brokerage account (this is known as a margin loan), be very careful. Borrowing limits are usually 50% of the account value. If your margined security takes a tumble on the market, your broker will require more cash or collateral to maintain your loan.

CONFUSED? STRANGLED BY LOOPHOLES AND RED TAPE?

If you're running into snags or all these techniques are confusing or require too much research, then request our free brochure *We Can Help* (Octameron, PO Box 2748, Alexandria, VA 22301). It describes our college admission and financial aid services. Neither cost very much and both can save you a bundle—both in money and in time.

Our Tuesday Special. We keep an experienced counselor on the phone nearly every Tuesday from 10 AM until 4 PM EST, to answer questions you may have about college financing (or selection or admission). The conversation will cost you $30 which you may charge against your VISA or MASTER CARD. Call (703) 836-5480.

Chapter 8

Long-Range Planning:
College Is Still Years Away

COLLEGE IS STILL YEARS AWAY

You've seen them. Charts that tell parents they have to save $800 a month from now until their newborn turns 18 if they want to afford college in the year 2012 (to say nothing of the savings requirements for families with two or three children). You are best advised to ignore these charts and any other "scare-the-pants-off-you" marketing strategy employed by organizations who, of course, will be pleased to help you save (and invest) that $800 per month. Instead, you should save as much money as you can afford, do it systematically, but be realistic, and remember, when your student enters college, your savings can be supplemented by a contribution from your earnings, their earnings and a manageable loan. If you feel you absolutely must use one of those "How Much You'll Need to Save" charts — a better goal might be to save enough to cover half the cost of college (also remember, you don't have to have the entire amount saved by the time your student first enrolls. He or she will be there for at least four years...make certain this expanded time frame is reflected in the chart's numbers). Still nervous? Think about buying a $200,000 home. Do you wait until you've saved the entire $200,000? Or do you think in terms of saving enough for the downpayment?

RULE OF 72

For novice investors, the Rule of 72 is a quick way to see how fast your money will grow. If you divide 72 by your investment's expected rate of return, the resulting answer is the length of time it will take for your money to double. For example, your $10,000 investment is earning 6%. In twelve years (72/6) it will be worth $20,000. At 8%, your $10,000 will equal $20,000 in just nine years.

TAX PLANNING VS. COLLEGE AID

When college is still years away, the name of the game is to accumulate enough money to help with the inevitable bills. Unfortunately, plans to minimize tax liability frequently run counter to plans to maximize financial aid eligibility — making decisions about saving money even more complex.

Example 1: The first decision a family must make is whether to save money in the parents' or the child's name. For tax purposes, unearned income derived from parental assets can be assessed at a higher rate than unearned income from a child's assets. (For children under 14, the first $600 in interest or dividend income is tax-free. The next $600 is taxed at the child's rate. And any unearned income in excess of $1,200 is taxed at the parents's rate.) For financial aid purposes, however, parental assets are assessed at no more than 5.6% while student assets are assessed at a flat 35%. This often wipes out all the tax advantages previously received. The lesson? If there's any chance the family will qualify for financial aid, save in the parents's name.

Example 2: For tax purposes, many families consolidate their debt using a home equity loan (which then decreases the equity in their home) so that their interest payments can remain deductible, saving their cash for other expenses. For financial aid purposes, some people use cash to pay down their mortgage (thus increasing the equity in their homes), because home equity is not a reportable asset on the federal student aid form. The lesson? If there's any chance the family is going to qualify for financial aid, look closely at the positioning of assets well in advance of filing the aid application.

GETTING GOOD FINANCIAL ADVICE

Where do you go to get good advice on maximizing savings, both for college and for retirement? Some people get all the information they need by clipping articles from consumer-oriented personal finance magazines like *Kiplinger's, Money, Smart Money, Fortune,* and *Forbes.* Other people rely on a stockbroker for advice about the marketplace, an accountant for tax strategies, and an attorney for the latest on trusts and estates. Between these three groups of professionals, families can get a lot of sound advice on financial planning. There is, however, an emerging group of professionals who should be able to combine the advice you get from your broker, your accountant and your lawyer — that is the certified financial planner. Before hiring a CFP, however, make certain to re-read the advice about financial planners in Chapter 1, and ask questions!

SAVINGS PHILOSOPHIES

Ask ten financial advisors to recommend the best way to save for college and you're likely to get ten very different answers. First, you must decide how the money should be saved — in the parents' name? the child's name? a trust? Then you must decide how much risk you're willing to take with your money.

It's very difficult to offer sound investment advice in a vacuum, i.e., without knowing how much risk a family is comfortable with taking. As a general rule, the safer the investment option, the lower the return. The riskier the option, the greater the return (as well as the potential for a huge loss). Most of the plans described in this chapter are safe.

How can you tell if your portfolio is too risky? Simple, if you consistently wake up in the middle of the night concerned about a price drop in your stock or bond fund, you should rethink the composition of your portfolio.

SAMPLE PORTFOLIOS

The composition of your portfolio should change with the age of your children. When they are young, you can afford to take more risks than you can when tuition bills are just around the corner. Here's one example:

The Early Years (Under 6). About 90% of your money should be in stock funds, split between aggressive growth (the most risky) and growth and income (less risky). The other 10% should be in something safe like a money market or CD.

The Middle Years (6 to 13). You should keep about 90% in stock funds, but shift the money out of aggressive growth and into more conservative growth and income.

The Pre-College Years (14 to 17). According to personal finance expert Jane Bryant Quinn, money you'll need within four years shouldn't be invested in a mutual fund, because historically, that's how long it takes for stocks to drop from a peak and rise back to the original price. Our advice? During these years, aim to keep 50% of your money in a growth and income fund, and start moving the rest (over the next four years) into CDs or a money market.

PAY YOURSELF FIRST

The best way to accumulate money is to pay yourself first, and use an investment strategy called Dollar-Cost-Averaging. The premise is simple. You have a fixed amount of money withheld from your paycheck each month and invest that money in something like a mutual fund; you don't have to worry about whether the market is up or down, and you're pretty certain to be safe from financial disaster. In fact, you'll probably do better than most professional fund managers. Why does this work? Let's say you have $200 withheld from your paycheck and wired into a brokerage account each month where it buys shares of your favorite mutual fund. When the market is up, your $200 buys relatively fewer shares than when the market is low, so the average cost of your shares is lower than the average price during the period.

Monthly Investment	Price per Share	Shares Purchased
$200	$25	8.00
$200	$25	8.00
$200	$30	6.66
$200	$25	8.00
$200	$20	10.00
$200	$25	8.00
Totals $1,200	$150	48.66

Your average cost per share is $24.66 ($1,200/48.66) while the average market price per share is $25 ($150/6). You win! Here's another way to look at your smart investment: Had you simply purchased 8 shares each month, you would have only 48 shares for your $1,200. Now you have 48.66. You win again! This method of regular, systematic savings will allow you to accumulate funds fast, especially if you start when your children are very young!

CUSTODIAL ACCOUNTS AND TRUSTS

Families that want to save money in the child's name have two main choices — custodial accounts and trusts.

Custodial Accounts under the Uniform Gift to Minors Act (UGMA) accept money. Custodial accounts under the Uniform Transfer to Minors Act (UTMA) also accepts property. Both are irrevocable gifts to a child where a custodian is responsible for managing the funds until the minor reaches the age of majority. The money which accumulates does so under the minor's lower tax liability. UGMA and UTMA accounts are easy to set up (just call your banker or broker), but they have one major drawback. Once the funds are turned over (as early as age 18), the child can do whatever he or she wants with them. Pay for college, pay for a new car, pay for a lifetime supply of jelly donuts...Individuals may make a tax-free gift worth up to $10,000 to either of these two accounts

Minority Trust. Under section 2503(c) of the tax code, families can establish an inter-vivos (living) trust for a minor, provided the funds are used solely for the benefit of that minor. This trust has one main advantage over a UGMA. The trustee has control over the funds until the "donee" is 21 years old — well into the college paying years

Crummey Trust. Named for the court case under which it originated, this is very similar to the 2503(c) trust described above, but with one important exception. The recipient of the trust (presumably your child) may withdraw any contributions made to the trust in that year. If your child makes no withdrawals, the contribution is added to the principal (and if your child does something stupid with the money, you can stop adding to the trust). The trust may continue as long as the trustee chooses.

Individuals may also each make a tax-free gift of up to $10,000 to either of these two trusts. The drawbacks? You'll need an attorney, and as much as $2,500 in attorney fees to set up a trust and, you'll have to file separate income tax returns for them. Worst of all, last year's tax law changes resulted in trust income being taxed far more heavily than individual income. The idea was to nab the rich. Unfortunately, many of the affected trusts are those set up to care for the disabled or to pay for college. Unless there's a quick change, the first $1,500 in trust income is taxed at 15%; the next $2,000 is taxed at 28%; the next $2,000 is taxed at 31%, the next $2,000 at 36% and anything above $7,500 is taxed at 39.6%.

Charitable Remainder Unitrust. You donate a set amount of money (usually at least $20,000) to a college or a charitable institution, such as your alma mater or the American Association of University Women, but stipulate that from 5% or 10% of the value of the gift, be paid out each year into a custodial account established for your college-bound student. At the end of a designated time frame, the principal goes to the college or charity. Meanwhile, you, the donor have (1) had a substantial tax deduction (2) built a college fund for junior and (3) given money to a favored charity. Many people choose to donate an appreciated asset for the trust to sell, because that way they avoid paying tax on the appreciation, yet they get to deduct the full market value of the item. You'll need professional help to set up such a trust.

CDS AND T-BILLS
Some of the safest, and easiest ways for parents to save money are through short- and long-term Certificates of Deposit (CDs), Treasury bills (which mature in 13, 26 or 52 weeks), Treasury notes (which mature in 1 to 10 years), Treasury bonds (which mature in 10 to 30 years), and US savings bonds. As you shop around for rates, remember brokerage firms usually offer the highest rates on CDs and money-market funds. As of this writing, you can get six-month CDs that yield 4.23%, 26-week T-bills at 4.5%, two-year Treasury notes at 5.87%, five-year notes at 6.58%, ten-year notes at 7.01%, and 30-year Treasury bonds at 7.26%.

GOVERNMENT BONDS
Parents who have purchased US EE savings bonds will not have to pay any tax on the interest that accrues, provided the bonds are used to pay for their children's education. Full benefits are available to couples with incomes of $70,350 or less and to single parents with incomes of $46,900 or less when it's time to redeem their bonds. The exemption will taper off for families with incomes above these limits, and disappear completely for couples with incomes above $100,350 and single parents with incomes above $61,900. Income limitations will be indexed for inflation, so, by the time you redeem your bonds, the income ceilings may be much higher. One Catch: Your income for the year in which you plan to redeem your bonds includes all the interest the bonds have earned! This additional income may push some families right past the income cut-offs and ironically eliminate their exclusion! Bonds may be purchased at any time during the year, but the purchasers must be at least 24 years of age. In other words, families with incomes too high to benefit from the tax break may not have their children take advantage of the benefit by buying the bonds themselves. For the same reason, grandparents and couples who file separate tax returns are also ineligible to participate. Families holding the bonds for at least five years are guaranteed a rate of at least 4%. Rates are adjusted twice a year (May 1 and November 1). The current rate is 4.7%. Bonds are available through payroll deductions and at most banks and credit unions. For more information, get a copy of *The Savings Bond Question and Answer Book* and *Questions and Answers About Education Savings Bonds* from the Department of Treasury, US Savings Bonds Division, Washington, DC 20226.

MUTUAL FUNDS
The best way for small investors to play the market is via a mutual fund. By having your money pooled with money from lots of other investors, you gain the advantage of diversification and professional fund management. Mutual funds are usually catego-rized by their investment goals. For example, *Growth Funds* aim to increase the value of your investment rather than provide you with a large stream of dividends. Growth Funds generally invest in stocks and are best suited for people who plan to hold on to the fund for a longer period of time, for example, people who won't need to tap their college fund for many years. *Income Funds* focus on providing investors with high current income (i.e., large dividends). Income funds generally invest in corporate bonds, the federal government, and state and local governments. They bring higher yields than money market funds, but their share price can move up or down, making them a little riskier. *Money Market Funds* are very safe, and accordingly, offer the

investor the lowest return. Money Market Funds generally invest in high quality securities with short maturities (e.g., bank CDs, US Treasury bills). Other types of funds include hybrids of the above, for example, Aggressive Growth, Balanced Growth, and Growth and Income. Investors will also find specialty funds grouped by company type (for example, energy, financial services, health care, etc.). For a directory (and overview) of thousands of mutual funds, send $5.00 to the Investment Company Institute, PO Box 66140, Washington DC 20035-6140. You can either buy funds yourself (using information from this directory, the *Wall Street Journal*, or consumer magazines like *Smart Money, Kiplinger's* or *Money*) or, work with a broker.

This tip from the *WSJ*: To simplify your taxes, you might set up four separate funds. Then, to cover each year's college expenses, sell one fund. Also remember, as students approach college age, families should lower their investment risk by shifting the balance of their savings from aggressive growth funds to growth and income funds, and finally, to money market funds.

ZERO COUPON BONDS

These are essentially municipal bonds, corporate bonds, and treasury bonds stripped of their interest coupons. Owners receive no income while holding the bonds. Instead, the income is compounded semi-annually and re-invested. At some time in the future, you receive a fixed sum that is considerably larger than your purchase price. Let's use an example—a 10% municipal bond. That bond, if it matures in 2002, will cost you $485 per thousand, which means you pay $4,850 today to get $10,000 eight years from now. A $10,000 bond maturing in thirteen years will cost you $2,810. And, if you buy bonds the day your child is born, you can get a $10,000 bond maturing in eighteen years for only $1,730.

Zero coupons are often not called "zero coupons." Instead, investors should look for them under acronyms like STRIPS (Separate Trading of Registered Interest and Principal of Securities), TIGRS (Treasury Investment Growth Receipts), CATS (Certificates of Accrual on Treasury Securities), and M-CATS (with "M" standing for Municipal).

Many families like to use zero coupon bonds to save for college expenses because they can time the maturity dates to coincide with their students' tuition bills. Also, they know exactly how much money they will receive when those tuition bills come due.

There are, however, several drawbacks to zero coupon bonds, which families should be aware of before making this type of long-term monetary investment.

- Corporate bonds and municipal bonds may be called before they reach maturity, and if you miss the call, you may be in for a nasty surprise when you go to claim your money. Here's why. When a bond is called (usually because of declining interest rates) interest stops accumulating, and its value, therefore, freezes. The $10,000 face value you thought you were receiving could turn out to be little more than the bond's original cost (which may have been only a few thousand dollars). Treasury bonds are much safer, as they carry a no-call provision.
- Even though no income is distributed, tax must be paid yearly on the accrued interest. The exception is for zero-coupon municipals which are tax free (but somewhat rare).
- There is no way of knowing with any certainty what the value of the money will be when the bond matures. If interest rates rise, the value of the bond drops. If interest rates drop, the value of the bond rises. As a rule, corporate bonds have the highest yield, but also carry the highest risk.
- Investors take the risk that the issuer of their bond will be around in 20 years to pay off the amount due. To be safe, avoid municipal bonds issued by small municipalities and corporate bonds with risky ratings (AAA is good, DDD is not). To be extra safe, buy mutual-fund corporate zeros or government backed Treasury zeros.

LIFE INSURANCE

Many people are completely (and justifiably) confused by the endless variety of life insurance options. We recommend you be very careful about using cash value life insurance to save for college—only use it when you're certain to maintain the policy for a long time, otherwise fees and commissions make the surrender value worth little more than your initial investment. If you're speaking to an insurance agent, ask the most questions about "variable life." Of the three types of cash value life insurance (the other two are "whole life" and "universal life"), it gets the best reviews from consumer-oriented investment writers. It is, however, the riskiest and if you can't invest for at least 15 years, it's unlikely that compounding will ever make the investment worthwhile.

In any case, don't decide to invest in life insurance while under pressure or because of tax laws or financial aid rules that place the value of your insurance outside the need analysis formula. First, be certain you compare three things—the costs of the contract (monthly charges, first year charges, front-end loads and surrender penalties); the performance of the funds in the contract (ask to see the returns after all costs have been deducted); and the cost of the life insurance coverage. Second, be certain you're comparing apples and apples. If someone shows you comparisons making one company's policy look significantly better than another's, be certain both were calculated using the same market assumptions (for example, reasonable and supportable rates of return, mortality rates and expenses). Finally, buy only from highly rated companies (Look for A. M. Best reports in your library for ratings of the insurance industry).

Insurance companies also offer Certificates of Annuity, which are very much like Certificates of Deposit (CDs), except the interest your money earns will be tax-deferred. Certificates come in one, three, and five year terms. The interest rate is guaranteed through to maturity. Sometimes you can withdraw up to 10% of your investment each year without penalty. And sometimes you can borrow up to 75% of the value of the contract.

Prospective buyers of life insurance might consider a service offered by the National Insurance Consumer's Organization. For a fee (around $35), NICO will analyze a policy and help you compare it to others. NICO, 121 North Payne Street, Alexandria, VA 22314, or call 703/549-8050.

Some insurance companies will also provide you with advice on college selection and financing. Although their goal is generally to sell you insurance products (if you need them), the planning service is free, as is the phone call: American National Life Insurance (800/777-2372) and Occidental Life Insurance (800/334-4324) both sponsor Collegiate Planning Centers, and will refer you to lenders for the Stafford Loan.

CATTLE FUTURES

Just kidding. Hillary may have parlayed $1,000 into $100,000 over ten short months, but the commodities market is a little too volatile and way too mysterious for this brief an overview of investment strategies.

INNOVATION

Keep your eyes open for new, innovative savings plans. Most large banks and insurance companies realize a lot of money can be made by "helping" families save for college, and are becoming increasingly innovative (and competitive) in their offerings. Weigh the plans carefully and look for hidden charges. Make certain you know the effective rate of return on your investment, not just the coupon rate or the interest rate. Here is one example of innovation:

NIKE will match a percentage of each employee's savings provided the savings be used for their child's future education. Participants may deposit up to $1,000 per year per child beginning when the child enters 9th grade. NIKE matches 25% to a maximum of $250 per year.

The College Savings Bank in Princeton sells CDs based on the average cost (room, board tuition and fees) of 500 independent colleges. The interest rate is 1.5% lower than the average annual tuition increase at these colleges. In other words, if the index rises by 7.61%, the interest rate is 6.11%. Your upfront premium reduces the effective rate of your investment a percentage or so more, making the actual yield not that much higher than that offered by most passbook savings accounts. Participants in this plan also face steep penalties for early withdrawal; 10% of principal during the first three years, 5% thereafter. Plan originators realize investors could do better elsewhere, but like proponents of all prepaid tuition plans, what they are selling is security. Over time, families are assured that their CD will keep pace with college expenses, and that's not necessarily a bad way to invest. For more information CollegeSure CDs, call 1-800-888-2723.

Tuition Access (in Chicago) is developing a credit card incentive plan much like the ones used by major airlines. Instead of earning frequent flier miles for each dollar spent, you'd start accruing money for an eventual rebate on the cost of college.

IN WHOSE NAME—PARENT OR CHILD?

As we mentioned earlier, the critical decision you must make, in any long-range capital accumulation plan, is whether the plan will be in your name, at your tax rate, or in the child's name, at the child's tax rate. The money will grow more quickly in the child's name because of the lower tax bracket. But when it comes time to pay tuition bills, the child's money is subject to a much heavier assessment. Colleges will demand 35% of the child's assets each year, but only 5.6% of parental assets.

Let's attach some numbers. A family in the 35% bracket (this includes an allowance for state taxes) elects to make a yearly gift of $1,000 to a child, starting at birth. The money is invested at 8%. At the end of eighteen years, the kitty will be worth $34,892. Had the family added $1,000 per year to a parental account, also invested at 8%, the money, under higher taxation, would have grown to only $28,662.

Now it's need analysis/family contribution time. For each of the next four years, the student's kitty is depleted by 35% of its value. The parental kitty, on the other hand, is depleted by only 5.6%. At the end of four years, the child's kitty has shrunk by $28,664 to $6,228. The parental kitty has shrunk by only $5,904 and is still a respectable $22,758.

So what should you do?

If there is no chance your family will qualify for aid, save in the child's name, the money will accumulate more quickly. To take advantage of the fact that unearned income of children over 14 is still taxed at the child's rate, if you have young children, your gifts should take the form of tax-deferred investments, such as US Savings Bonds and fast growing stocks. Once the child reaches 14, redeem the bonds, sell the stocks, and place the proceeds in a safe, but high yielding investment.Then spend it all on tuition.

If there is any chance for getting aid, save in the parent's name, make the smaller family contribution, and pad your college expenditures with need based aid.

Predicting aid eligibility is no easy task. Constantly changing tax laws and student assistance laws confuse professionals, to say nothing of those whose jobs do not depend on keeping up with Congressional activity. Here's what we advise. Assume the ratio between present earnings and assets and present college costs will hold for the future. Run your family through the Federal Methodology in Appendix 1. Compare the estimated family contribution with the current costs of colleges of interest. If your family contribution is less than the cost of college today, you may qualify for aid in the future. Remember to divide the parental contribution component by the number you will have in college at least half-time (including parents) at any one time.

Part IV
The Major Money Sources

Chapter 9
The Colleges

RETHINKING YOUR IDEAS ABOUT ADMISSION

Unless you plan to attend one of the few remaining highly selective colleges, rid yourself of the thought that it's hard to get into college. It's easy. Over 90% of all students are accepted by their first or second choice school.

In the old days, you applied to five or six schools; one or two where your odds were fifty-fifty, a couple where you had the edge, and a fall-back school that was sure to accept you. Today your selection strategy needs to be based on factors other than the possibility of rejection. First and foremost you should consider the quality of education offered by each institution and your fit with each institution, but then you should consider the financial aid offerings. Look for:

1. Schools with innovative payment plans. These can ease your cash flow problems.
2. Schools with innovative aid programs. These can channel money toward "desirable" students.
3. Schools with mountains of cash. These can usually handle your "need."
4. Schools with a reputation for leadership in your selected field of study. They are likely to be well-endowed in your field.

Next you should remember that financial aid resources are limited. The first people in line are more likely to have their need met than the last. Also, the intense competition for quality students translates into "no-need" awards and "preferential packaging." Lastly, financial aid administrators have some elbow room or leeway to reassess family contributions, costs of attendance, and the contents of aid packages.

Given these words of wisdom, it's up to you to take action.

1. Apply "early decision" for both admission and financial aid—that way you should have all your need met.
2. Apply to colleges where your qualifications place you in the upper 25% of the applicant pool. That standing will have a significant impact on the composition of your aid package. Schools make no bones about that. In fact, one school described its preferential packaging policies in its catalogue. "With a GPA of 3.6 and combined SATs of 1200 or more, your need will be met 80% by scholarships, 15% by loans and 5% by work. But with a GPA below 3.3 and SATs below 1050, the package will contain only 10% in scholarships, 65% in loans and 25% in work."
3. Always pair your applications. For better "leverage," apply to two four-star schools; and two three-star schools; not just one of each. This may increase your number of non-refundable application fees, however, when you receive acceptances from schools of similar prestige, you may be able to play one against the other to improve your aid package. A school may not mind losing you to a lesser regarded college. But it will fight to keep you from going to a competitor.

IT DOESN'T HURT TO ASK

You'll often find the financial aid sections of college catalogues to be very vague. Pious generalities usually outnumber hard facts while the structure emphasizes modifiers and contradictions—the writers' skill with the double negative surpassing even the most convoluted legalese. Why do schools do this? First of all, it's very hard to be precise about financial aid when you know Uncle Sam will release some enormous rule change two days after 500,000 copies of your school's catalogue comes back from the printer. Second, financial aid decisions vary from student to student depending on the family's income and asset situation and the student's admission qualifications.

There are exceptions. Andrews University (MI) once called its aid philosophy the "stretch concept." You stretch and Andrews stretches. The University of Pittsburgh at Bradford (PA) uses Looney Tunes-like characters to help you make sense of all the programs (if nothing else, their financial aid bulletin is actually fun to read). And Central College (IA) made no bones about using aid for recruiting. "Frankly, we're out to attract talented and academically-ambitious students and we'll reward them for their past performance as well as for their potential."

But such candor is seldom found. To get answers, you will have to write. Don't be bashful about writing. This is a buyer's market and you have the right to ask the colleges as many questions as they ask you. Your letter should raise questions about the availability of innovative payment and tuition aid plans of the type illustrated in the next two sections. And you should certainly obtain answers to the following questions:

1. Do you guarantee to meet a student's financial need (or a certain percentage of a student's need)? Reason: Under the Federal Methodology, many more families will be eligible for financial aid. Unfortunately, additional federal money is not likely to be appropriated to help all these newly eligible families.
2. Do you have a per-student-limit on the aid you provide? Reason: Some schools set ceilings, such as a $2,000 per student maximum.
3. Do I have to demonstrate a minimum amount of need to qualify for aid? Reason: Some schools won't consider students for aid unless they have at least $500 need.
4. Do you have a standard "unmet need" figure for each aid recipient? Reason: Some schools will, automatically, leave each aid recipient $500 short.
5. What is your expected "student earnings" figure? Reason: Regardless of the results of need analysis, some colleges will expect a certain amount (which could be as high as $1,500 per year). The colleges will expect that amount, whether it comes from the student's contribution or the parents' contribution.
6. Is there an application cut-off date for guaranteeing a student's unmet need? Reason: Some colleges say they can meet all need for students whose applications are received prior to Date X. But no such guarantee extends to students who apply after the cut-off.
7. Do you maintain financial aid "waiting lists" or accept students on an "admit-deny" basis? Reason: These practices mean financially needy students are welcome but they will not receive financial aid.
8. If I don't apply for aid in my freshman year, can I apply in subsequent years? Reason: You can't be prohibited from applying, however, you may get nothing because many colleges give priority to "continuing recipients."
9. How are "outside scholarships" packaged? Reason: Different colleges have different "aid philosophies." For example, one school in New York will take the first $300 of the outside scholarship and 20% of the rest and use it to replace a loan. What's left reduces the student's grant from that school. At other colleges, the outside scholarship merely replaces, on a dollar for dollar basis, collegiate grants, causing the poet Leider to ponder from her garret:

> *You found a nifty scholarship*
> *To loosen the tuition grip.*
> *But does this change what you must pay?*
> *Or do they take your grant away?*

Don't expect an outside scholarship to be applied to your family contribution. According to federal regulations, no-need scholarships cannot be used in that manner (unless, as explained in Chapter 7, the scholarship exceeds the amount of your financial need). But do search for a policy that at least permits it to replace part of the package's self-help component (loans and work-study).

10. What percentage of alumni contribute to the school's annual fundraising campaign? Reason: If you are worried about the college's financial survival, you can't ask for a corporate balance sheet. But you can check with the college's development office to learn whether the school has strong alumni support. Here are some of the best: Randolph-Macon (VA), 62%, Dartmouth (NH), 65.5%; Siena (NY), 65.1%; Williams (MA), 63.6%; and Centre (KY), 60.1%. When colleges have this kind of loyalty, they are not going to fold.

As another yardstick, you might also ask about the size of the alumni donation per current enrolled student. Last year, Episcopal Theological Seminary of the Southwest and Goshen College grads gave the most, at $16,924 and $16,569 per current student enrolled, respectively. Rounding out the top twenty were Bridgewater, Randolph-Macon (Women's), California Institute of Technology, Yale, Wesleyan, Wabash, Swarthmore, Williams, Sweet Briar, Vassar, Wentworth Military Academy, DePauw, University of the South, Dartmouth , Smith, Washington and Lee, Simpson, and Mills. The amount per student at these schools ranged from $11,389 (Bridgewater) to $5,389 (Mills).

SEVENTEEN INNOVATIVE PAYMENT PLANS

1. **Installment Plans.** Realizing not many people can write a $5,000 or $10,000 check at the beginning of each semester, many colleges try to soften the blow by permitting you to spread the payments. Furthermore, by taking advantage of installment plans, you may not have to borrow as much for college as you originally thought. If a college doesn't have a plan of its own, ask whether it works with Academic Management Service (800-635-0120). AMS has contracts with nearly 1,500 schools, but sometimes you have to ask the right person the right question to find out. Here are the variants you may encounter.
   - Interest Policy: (1) No interest (2) Fixed interest (3) Interest on the remaining balance (4) No interest, but a one-time fee.
   - Down Payment Policy: (1) No down payment (2) Down payment of one-third or one-fourth.
   - Payment Frequency Policy: (1) Ten monthly installments (2) Two installments per semester (3) Four installments per semester.
   - A combination of these variants.
2. **Prepayment Discount.** Pay a year all at once, and your tuition is discounted, sometimes by as much as 10%.
3. **Advance Payment Bonus.** Place money into your account before it's due and the college will add a monthly bonus to your credit balance. It can be a set dollar amount (e.g., $100) or it can be a percentage of the amount on deposit (e.g., 2%).
4. **Adjustable Rate Loans.** First we had the adjustable rate mortgages; now colleges are offering adjustable rate tuition loans. Sometimes the amount of your monthly payment will change with the rate. Other times, however, the size of your monthly payment remains the same, but because neither the total amount borrowed nor interest rates can be predicted — both tuition costs and interest rates fluctuate — borrowers will not know how long they must make their payments. All they can be sure of is that the payments will continue long after graduation.
5. **Tuition Freezes.** A guarantee that tuition will hold for a set length of time or that it won't increase by more than a fixed percentage (e.g., 3%). Some schools invoke freezes to improve retention and limit them to 3rd and 4th years of attendance.
6. **Guaranteed Tuition Plans I.** No Prepayment. Guarantees students their tuition will not be increased in their sophomore, junior, and senior years.
7. **Guaranteed Tuition Plans II.** Deposit Required. Same as preceding plan, but the college requires you to maintain a set sum on deposit — anywhere from $500 to $3,000. These plans may a have a financing option.

8. **Guaranteed Tuition Plans III.** Prepayment Required. Pay four years tuition in advance, at the rate which prevails in your freshman year. Parents who have the resources to make an out-of-pocket prepayment must decide whether the tuition increases they will be spared are worth more than what their money could earn in interest if it had not been used for prepayment. If the money is to be borrowed, parents usually have two choices: (1) The sponsoring college will act as lender, offering the money at a favorable interest rate. Repayment, under such an arrangement, may extend from four to fifteen years. (2) Parents may consider raising the money by borrowing against the equity in their house. The interest rate may or may not be higher than the rate offered by the college. One advantage is that interest payments on home equity loans of up to $100,000 are tax deductible.

9. **Guaranteed Tuition Plans IV.** Other Types. At some schools, the guaranteed tuition plan covers as many years as parents can pay in advance — one, two, three, or four. At others, the school will sweeten the pot by rebating say 10% of the payment at the end of each year.

10. **Guaranteed Tuition Plan V.** Tuition Futures. Families can purchase four year tuition packages in one lump sum. The amount you pay depends upon when the student will enter the school. For example, parents of a three-year old might pay $5600 to cover four years worth of tuition beginning in the year 2009. One catch: If the student is not admitted or decides to go elsewhere, some schools refund only the initial investment, and keep the accumulated interest for themselves. Be sure to ask about this. Many schools, including the plan's originator, Duquesne (PA) have since abandoned it as state plans continue to get underway (see Chapter 11).

11. **Stretched Payments.** Not unlike a loan. Parents of students who do not qualify for aid defer a fixed amount of their tuition bill. They are given two years to pay the deferred amount and are charged a slight interest rate.

12. **Barter.** A usable service provided by you or your parents is exchanged for tuition.

13. **Three-Year Option.** The college offers a "time-shortened degree option" that permits students to satisfy graduation requirements in three years, saving one year in tuition costs.

14. **Two Degrees in One.** Students can also save a year's tuition by finding schools that offer joint undergraduate-graduate degree programs. For example, students can receive their BA-MBA in five years instead of the usual six, or a BA-MA in four years instead of the usual five.

15. **Choice of Accommodations and Meal Plans.** Do you need a spacious room with a spectacular view, or are you happy contemplating the backside of a dumpster? Do you need 21 meals a week in the college dining hall or would you rather cook for yourself when the daily special reads "Chef's Surprise or Mystery Meat?" Colleges are now giving you options. Some colleges have housing contracts that vary up to $2,000 per year, depending on location and type of room. Others offer several different meal plans. Cost difference: from $25 to $1,000 per year.

16. **Use of Credit Cards for Bill Payment.** Provides credit card holders with some flexibility but can cost them dearly in finance charges on unpaid monthly balances. If you pay by this option, you might consider using an "affinity" credit card that at least gives you a bonus, like frequent flier miles. Or, use the college's own card. Georgetown makes over $100,000 per year from its affinity cards, and ploughs the money back into scholarship programs.

17. **Use of Electronic Bank Transfers.** A set amount is transferred from your account to the college each month, without any human being ever touching the money.

THIRTY SIX INNOVATIVE STUDENT AID PROGRAMS

1. **Academic Scholarships.** Over 1200 colleges and universities offer scholarships — generally of the "no-need" type — to students who meet special excellence criteria in grade point averages, SAT/ACT scores, or class standing. See *The A's & B's of Academic Scholarships* (inside back cover)

2. **Low Interest Loans.** Many colleges have become low-interest lenders to offset Uncle Sam's yo-yo student aid policies and provide parents with certainty and stability in financial planning. The Consortium on Financing Higher Education, representing 32 selective, expensive, primarily East Coast colleges has organized a program called SHARE. Parents of students at any of the consortium schools can borrow up to $20,000 per year and take up to 20 years to repay. Borrowers may choose between a monthly, variable rate loan (the prime rate plus 2%) or a one-year renewable rate (the prime rate plus 3-4%). Families may defer payment of principal for up to four years while the student is enrolled. Other costs include a guarantee fee of 5% of the loan amount. For more information, call 800-634-9308.

3. **Quickie Loans.** Many colleges offer short term, small loans to tide students over in times of temporary financial crisis. These loans usually run from $100 to $500, but sometimes students can get up to $5,000.

4. **Replacing Loans.** Many schools will let you use outside scholarships to replace the loan component of your financial aid package. Some schools limit this bonus to bright students, or will convert your loan to a grant only if you maintain a certain GPA. Others will make the switch only if the student finds the scholarship before the loan processing begins. Students should also inquire if the school has a limit (e.g., $2,000) on the total amount it will replace.

5. **Middle Income Assistance Programs.** Special scholarships and loans for middle-income families.

6. **Asset-Rich Families.** Land-rich families whose holdings are "non-liquid" but disqualify them for assistance can sometimes get special consideration.

7. **Family Plans.** Rebates or lower tuitions when more than one family member attends the college. And that includes not only brother and sister, but also Mom, Dad and Grandma. Examples: Trinity College (DC) gives a 33% discount to additional family members. At Santa Clara (CA), the first of three enrolled at the same time gets free tuition, while Pace University (NY) lets the parents of enrolled undergrads take courses free on a space available basis.

8. **Alumni Children.** Tuition breaks for alumni kids are also common. Colleges like to establish multi-generation relationships with families. That's how chairs get endowed and buildings get donated.

9. **Peace of Mind.** A few schools will waive tuition payments in part or in full for any enrolled student should the person primarily responsible for the student's support die or suffer total disability.

10. **Incentives for Academic Achievement.** Many colleges have special scholarships and awards for the top enrolled (continuing) students. Other schools offer academic awards to any student who was in the top 10% of their high school class. Finally, some schools will convert part of a student's loans to grants if the student maintains a high GPA.

11. **Matching Scholarships.** Many schools will match church scholarships up to $500 or $1000. Other schools will match state regents awards, or Dollars for Scholars awards.

12. **Remissions for Student Leaders.** Many colleges will provide free tuition to campus leaders, for example, officers of the student government, editors of the school publications. Again, this won't happen to you on admission. But you should know about it so that you can get a head start on your campaign for student body president.

13. **Remissions for Work.** At Warren Wilson (NC) and Blackburn (IL) students get free room and board. But they must put in fifteen hours of campus work every week. Berea (KY) charges no tuition to students of limited means, but requires them to work ten hours/week. Many other schools provide room and board for residence hall assistants and supervisors. You may not qualify in your first year, but it's an opportunity you should know about.

14. **Emphasis on Student Employment.** Many colleges have beefed up their place-ment offices to help students find on- and off-campus employment. Here are some examples of especially noteworthy programs we've heard about over the past few years. Blufton College (OH) budgeted over $300,000 for campus employment in a "Learn & Earn" program. Princeton (NJ) assisted students who want to become entrepreneurs. Cornell (NY), in a massive program, offered over 400 students $2,000 work grants in the hope of reducing their dependence on loans. Schools like Amherst (MA) use their formidable alumni network to locate student summer work opportunities. St. Edward's University (TX) entered into an agreement with a major retail chain for hundreds of part-time jobs. A special benefit of this program: It conserves federal work-study funds.

15. **Off-Hour Rates.** Many colleges set lower credit hour charges for courses taken during off-hours—evenings, weekends and summers. The difference can be as high as $300 per course or a 50% reduction in room rates (for summer school).

16. **Recruiting Discount.** Bringing in another student can pay off. Some schools will reduce your tuition by as much as 10% for each of your recruits who enroll.

17. **Moral Obligation Scholarships.** Not a scholarship. Not a loan. The college provides money to the student and attaches a moral—but not legal—obligation to pay it back after graduation. A special sweetener: Until IRS changes its rules, the pay-back becomes a gift to the college and a tax deduction to the former student.

18. **Trial Attendance.** Some colleges say, "Try us you'll like us" and will offer new students a discount on their first few credits. For example, the school may offer free classes to high school juniors and seniors, it may let some students try the school for one semester for a low fee (e.g., $25), or it may run a free summer program to give students a little taste.

19. **Bucking the Trend.** Some colleges seek to win the enrollment competition by freezing or even lowering tuition.

20. **Special Scholarship Drives.** Some schools have launched special fund-raising drives aimed at increasing their in-house financial aid kitty. Columbia University (NY) raises $100,000 a year from Visa and Master card users through a collabora-tion with MBNA America Bank.

21. **Helping Students Find Scholarships.** Hundreds of schools have special offices to help students find grants, scholarships, etc.

22. **Older Student Remissions.** If you are over 24, some schools will give you a discount on tuition, however, at most school, "older" means 50 or 60. In fact, many public schools offer free tuition to senior citizens as long as they are state residents and attending on a space available basis.

23. **Special Students.** Colleges look for students with unique interests or back-grounds. Many give special scholarships to any member of the National Honor Society or students who want to be math or science teachers. Grand Canyon (AZ) is looking for Eagle Scouts. Tarleton State (TX) offers rodeo scholarships. And, Arkansas College (AR) will pay you to play the bagpipes.

24. **Retention Awards.** Retaining students is important to colleges. Some offer financial inducements to get you back each year such as cancelling part of your loans. Arkansas College (AR) offered an equally attractive gift to students who remained in good standing through their junior year; during January term of their senior year, the school would pay transportation and housing expenses for two weeks of foreign travel. What fun!

25. **Travel Awards.** Some schools want to repay you either for a campus visit or, if you are enrolled, for the distances you must travel to obtain your learning.

26. **Loan Origination Fee.** Stafford Loans carry a 3% origination fee. Some schools will pay your origination fee.

27. **Adopt-a-Student.** Some schools have convinced local churches and community groups to help students with scholarship money. Other schools work with local

businesses (some companies even extend interest-free loans to students that are forgiven if the student, after graduation, goes to work for the sponsor).

28. **Students Helping Students.** When that happens, it's a sign of good student morale and a friendly campus. Some examples we've heard about recently: At Azusa Pacific (CA), students raised $16,000 for scholarships in a phonathon. DePauw (IN) students did even better, raising $145,000. At Sarah Lawrence (NY), a scholarship auction netted $7,000. At Brown (RI), the University put $4 in the college's scholarship fund for every hour student volunteers spent picking up litter on campus. At Georgetown (DC) students have organized a credit union and at Guilford (NC) students have raised over $100,000 to start a loan fund of their own. At Notre Dame (IN) students waived return of room-damage deposits, electing to contribute the money to a scholarship fund. Fitchburg State (MA) deposited all parking fines in a scholarship fund. And Davidson's (NC) senior class gift to the college was a $100,000 scholarship fund.

29. **Running Start.** High school students can spend their senior year, or the summer before their senior year on a campus, taking regular college work. Colleges look on such students as a farm club. At Wesley (DE), any local student in the top 40% of the high school class (with combined SATs of at least 800) may take (and receive academic credit for) up to two courses each semester for free. Simon's Rock College (MA) awards 2-year scholarships to high school sophomores. After completing the two year "Acceleration to Excellence" program, students have the option of completing their BA at Simon's Rock for the cost of attending their home-state public university. No matter what program is offered, here are some questions to ask: Are the courses for college credit? If so, are the credits good only at the offering college or are they transferable?

30. **Help for the Unemployed.** Some schools offer free tuition to students from families whose major wage earner is unemployed.

31. **Free Tuition for Farmers.** Some schools offer up to a year of free tuition to farmers who have had to quit farming because of financial hardships.

32. **A Birthday Gift.** To celebrate its 100th anniversary, Dana (NE) let each of the school's 101 graduating seniors award a $4,000 scholarship to any new student who met Dana's admission requirements. Goucher (MD) also celebrated its 100th birthday. It did so by allowing selected students to attend college for four years at 1885 tuition rates, $100/year. Note: Both of these opportunities are past, but keep your eyes open for similar "celebrations."

33. **Guaranteed Degree.** Some schools allow graduates who are unhappy with their major (because they couldn't find a job, maybe) to return to the alma mater and major in another field, tuition-free, or at least at reduced tuition. One school, Saint Norbert College promises that if a student doesn't graduate in four years because the college failed to offer a required class, or a professor failed to give proper advice, the school will pay the additional tuition.

34. **Tuition Equalization.** To compete more effectively with public schools for top students, some private colleges offer their own tuition equalization programs. At Bard College (NY), first year students who were in the top ten of their high school class are charged only as much tuition as they would have paid had they gone to their state-supported school. The promise is good as long as they maintain a "B" average once in college.

35. **Toll-Free Numbers.** Hundreds of schools send financial aid recipients a toll-free number and the name of a "personal financial counselor" with whom to discuss financing options.

36. **Reward for Community Service.** The University of California, Berkeley (CA) will repay the federal loans of nearly 100 students who go into community or public service when they graduate. Brown U. (RI) has a $500,000 kitty to repay the loans of graduates who teach or work for public service agencies. Xavier U. (OH) gives five full cost scholarships to students who spend 15 hours a week providing

service leadership. The Washington Education Project lets college students earn academic credit for teaching nonreaders to read. Twelve schools currently participate, including New York University (NY) and Boston College (MA).

For a more complete listing of what colleges offer which programs, get *College CheckMate* (see inside back cover).

IMPACT OF TAX REFORM

Now that we've looked at the variety of innovative payment plans and student aid programs offered by our nations colleges, you must understand how their benefits are lessened by three provisions in the tax code:

1. **Interest on Consumer Debt is Not Deductible.** The deduction for interest paid on consumer debt (credit cards, auto loans, personal loans) has been phased out. This greatly diminishes the popularity of guaranteed tuition plans as the interest payments on the money most families must borrow to pay four years of tuition in advance is not deductible (unless the family borrows against its home. Interest on mortgage payments is still deductible). The non-deductibility of consumer debt also impacts on the desirability of using credit cards to pay tuition bills.

2. **Some Scholarships Taxed As Income.** The portion of a scholarship that exceeds tuition, fees, books and equipment is taxed as ordinary income. This means room and board scholarships may be taxed. If you've received a large grant, use it to pay the tax-free items first, and keep track of everything left over. You're usually on your own to report your good fortune to the IRS.

3. **Graduate Teaching Assistantships Taxed As Income.** Any tuition discounts (or tuition payments) received in exchange for services is considered taxable income. The University of Wisconsin-Madison (as reported by Jane Bryant Quinn) sums up graduate aid quite nicely: "Stipends for teaching assistantships are taxable because the work helps the school without being central to a student's studies. Stipends for research assistants are tax free because the research, while of interest to the student and the teacher, isn't necessary to the school. Fellowships are clean—no work, no tax."

THE RICH SCHOOLS

Rich schools generally have more funds available for student aid than poor schools. At some, the average need-based grant ranges from $10,000 to $15,000! Rich schools also have greater flexibility in making financial aid awards. It's their money, so they are better able to take individual circumstances into account than schools that dispense, in the main, public funds. Wealth can be judged in one of two ways: (1) Total endowment or (2) endowment per enrolled student. Here are schools with mountains of money:

Over $5 billion: Harvard.

Over $2 billion: Princeton, Yale, Stanford

Over $1 billion: Texas A&M University System, Columbia, U. of California System, Emory, MIT, Washington U, Northwestern, Rice, U. of Chicago, Cornell, U. of Pennsylvania, U. of Texas System.

Over $500 million: Notre Dame, Vanderbilt, U. of Michigan, Dartmouth, Johns Hopkins, New York U., Duke, U. of Southern California, U. of Rochester, U. of Virginia, CalTech, Rockefeller U., Brown, Case Western.

Over $300 million: Ohio State, Wellesley, Macalester, U. of Delaware, Swarthmore, Smith, Southern Methodist, Loyola (Chicago), Boston College, Grinnell, Carnegie-Mellon, Texas Christian, U. of Cincinnati, Wake Forest, U. of Pittsburgh, Williams, Pomona, Indiana U., U. of Richmond, U. of Minnesota, Berea, U. of Tulsa, George Washington, Georgetown, Trinity. (TX), Boston U., Lehigh, Amherst, Wesleyan, Kansas U., Baylor and Middlebury.

Endowment per student leads to different rankings. Rockefeller U., $3,994,310; Princeton, $372,691; Harvard, $247,309; CalTech, $235,860; Rice, $218,396; Grinnell, $217,396; Swarthmore, $207,802; Yale, $196,960.

LEADERSHIP IN SELECTED FIELDS

Colleges that are acknowledged leaders in selected disciplines (e.g., the Midwestern colleges in agriculture; the western schools in mining and geology) are usually heavily endowed by private sponsors in the areas of their special expertise. You are far more likely to find an agriculture scholarship at Iowa State than at Baruch College in New York City, or a petroleum engineering scholarship at the University of Oklahoma than at the University of the District of Columbia.

For opinions on who is best in what, ask the guidance office or school library to pick up a copy of **Rugg's Recommendations on the Colleges** ($18.95, Rugg's Recommendations, 7120 Serena Court, Atascadero, CA 93422) or **The Gourman Report** (separate volumes for undergraduate and graduate programs, $14.95 each from Dearborn Trade, 800-245-BOOK. Another (perhaps better) way to get this kind of information is to speak with people you respect in your intended academic/career field. Find out where they went to school, and ask if they have any recommendations.

A tip: Very strong departments usually have scholarship funds they control themselves rather than the financial aid office. If you plan to major in a field in which a school is strong, consider dropping a note to the department head and ask about the possibility of departmental assistance.

WORKING WITH FINANCIAL AID ADMINISTRATORS

The median salary of financial aid directors, in 1993/94, was $42,300. You might want to keep that sum in mind as you get ready to explain how your $75,000 income has been ravaged by inflation to the point of making it impossible—absolutely impossible—to handle your family contribution.

Remember that financial aid administrators primarily dispense public funds—tax money—and such expenditures are usually quite controlled by law and regulations. Financial aid administrators do have some flexibility in awarding the colleges' own funds and in treating changed circumstances—such unfortunate events as death, disability, disaster, and divorce. If you feel that any element of your award letter—the student's expense budget, your family contribution, or the mix of aid programs offered—should be changed, then go ahead and call the office. But do so with sound reasons and, if necessary, with documentation. Don't take the approach that you're cutting a deal. Financial aid administrators are professionals working with limited funds. If they agree to increase your award, it's frequently at the expense of another's. The FAA will not make that decision lightly, and never without good cause. So before you bully your way into the financial aid office demanding a recount, document your case carefully and keep in mind that one catches more Drosophila Melanogaster with honey than with vinegar.

Chapter 10
Uncle Sam

Every Student's Song

Do not forsake me, oh my Uncle, before commencement day.
Do not change programs, oh my Uncle, oh please, oh please — I say.
I do not know what costs await me, I only know there will be more.
I need to have the grants you give me, or be a drop-out, a lazy drop-out,
Or a starving sophomore.

MEET YOUR UNCLE—UNCLE SAM

It's hard to meet college costs without also meeting Uncle Sam. For many students, applying for financial aid represents their first encounter with Uncle Sam.

One thing will become apparent very quickly. Getting things from Uncle Sam is no more pleasant an experience than giving him things, like your money at tax time. Here is what you should expect:

Uncle Sam likes forms. Lots of forms. Most of the forms have an awkward layout, an illogical sequence, and poorly written instructions for filling them out.

Uncle Sam makes a sharp distinction between "authorizations" and "appropriations." A program may be authorized, but that doesn't mean a nickel will be spent (appropriated) for it. Be careful when you hear about a much-heralded $10 billion student aid program. Before your expectations get too high, make sure the money for the program has actually been appropriated.

Uncle loves semantics and fine distinctions. His authorization bill may promise a chicken in every pot. But the enabling legislation, usually expressed in regulations, may define "chicken" as "any part of the bird," a claw, a feather... Or the definition may emphasize the avian nature of a chicken. The operative word then becomes "bird" and any bird can be substituted for a chicken — pigeon, crow...

Uncle is a social engineer. After redefining chicken, he will turn his attention to the pot. He may rule that anybody who owns a pot large enough to hold a chicken is too rich to qualify for a fowl. Only owners of small pots can get birds — the smaller the pot, the bigger the bird will seem.

Uncle's promises don't hold for very long. Any program can be supplemented, altered, filibustered, modified or rescinded in mid-year or near election time when it becomes important to hold down expenses and balance the budget.

Uncle likes to arm wrestle with himself. If the Administration doesn't like what Congress has mandated (or vice versa), it will delay, miss deadlines, base its case on budget figures that had already been rejected (but not yet replaced), blow smoke over the issues, hold up regulations, or tie up appropriated funds.

Uncle's timing does not correspond to the academic cycle. When you want to start planning for the next year, usually in September, Uncle is not ready for you. By the time he can tell you what he will do for you, you've already made your plans.

But when all is said and done, Uncle Sam is still your main source of financial aid. Warts or no warts, you had better learn to live with him and like him.

Program	Level of Study		Need-Based		Part-Timers		Need Analysis
	Under-grad	Grad	Yes	No	Yes	No	
Pell Grant	X		X		X		FM
Stafford Loan	X	X	X			X	FM
PLUS Loans	X			X		X	none
Direct Stafford Loan	X	X	X			X	FM
Direct Plus Loan	X			X		X	none
Unsubsidized Stafford	X	X		X		X	FM
SEOG	X		X		X		FM
CW-S	X	X	X		X		FM
Perkins Loans	X	X	X		X		FM

THE BIG SIX TODAY

Most of Uncle's student aid flows through six gigantic programs. Three are student based — the Federal Pell Grant, the Federal Family Education Loan (Stafford and PLUS), and the Federal Direct Student Loan (Direct Stafford and Direct PLUS). You apply for assistance under these programs and the money comes to you.

The other three programs — Federal Supplemental Educational Opportunity Grants, Federal Work-Study and Federal Perkins Loans — are campus-based. That means, Uncle funds the programs, but gives the money to the colleges. The colleges, in turn, dispense the money to students in accordance with federal guidelines.

Uncle Sam also has some smaller grant programs that are state-based — The Paul Douglas Teacher Scholarship, The Robert C. Byrd Honors Scholarship, and National Science Scholars. Uncle funds the programs, but gives the money to the states to distribute (again, in accordance with federal guidelines).

Program information is available by calling **The Federal Student Aid Information Center,** 800-4-FED-AID, Monday through Friday between 9:00 a.m. and 5:30 p.m. (Eastern Time). The hearing-impaired may call 800-730-8913. Trained staff is available to assist families in completing financial aid applications, to explain the Expected Family Contribution, to answer questions about student eligibility, and to expedite loan payment problems. The number is NOT to be used for family financial counseling, to change information in your file, to make policy, or to expedite application processing.

If you suspect fraud, waste or abuse involving Federal student aid funds, please call the Education Department's Inspector General's Office at (800)MIS-USED. You may remain anonymous, if you wish.

Uncle publishes a free booklet called **The Student Guide: Financial Aid from the US Department of Education.** Sometimes budget constraints cause it to be replaced with a 12-page fact sheet. In either case, you can request a copy (usually after the first of the year) by calling 800-4-FED-AID.

PELL GRANTS

These are Uncle's largest gift program. Over $6.3 billion in Pells will be dispensed to 3.7 million students in 1995/96. They are the foundation of student aid, the bottom layer of the financial aid package. But they can also be called Pinochio Grants. Why? Because Uncle seldom holds to the award range that he promises. Last year, $2,400 became $2,300; in another year, $1,800 became $1,750. How does this happen? Easy. Uncle fails to request enough funds and then explains, unconvincingly, that more students applied to the program than he had expected. To solve this annual budget snafu, Congress will probably start capping the number of Pells, say at 3.93 million; after those awards are distributed, that's it, the money's gone. While it's sad that Pell may no longer be a full entitlement, a 3.93 million cap should not result in any students (who apply on time) from being turned down for money. Lesson: Apply early, just in case.

So what will the award range be for 1995/96? Our prediction: Pay no attention to last year's authorization bill that says Pells can go up to $4,100, and expect the range to remain $400 to $2,300 (or maybe $2,340 as Uncle has ever so generously proposed). Why are we so pessimistic? Until we come close to balancing our budget, Pell will not be fully funded. Remember the difference between "authorization" and "appropriation."

How large a Pell will you get? It depends on your EFC, the cost of education at your school and whether you're a part-time or full-time student. Uncle publishes "look-up" tables with exact levels of Pell funding, but to get an estimate, if your cost of education exceeds the maximum Pell (e.g., $2,300), just subtract your family contribution from the maximum grant. For example, a family contribution of $1,000 will translate into a grant of $1,300. For a detailed description of the program, please read *Loans and Grants From Uncle Sam* (see inside back cover).

Important: You apply for a Pell by completing the FAFSA. Make certain to go this route, even if you're certain you won't be eligible for the grant. Colleges and the states expect you to do so and won't consider you eligible for other awards until after they know your Pell status. The only way for them to know your Pell status is by seeing it on your Student Aid Report.

Things to Know About Pell Grants:

- About 30% of all FAFSAs will be verified by the college financial aid office. That's when you have to produce copies of income tax forms and other documents for a comparison check. These returns are selected for verification based on "preestablished criteria." That's bureaucratese for "something smells fishy."
- If you are a part-time, half-time or three-quarter time student, you receive 25%, 50% or 75% of your award, respectively.
- If there is a drastic change in your personal or financial circumstances after you have applied, let your financial aid administrator know. He or she will probably make an adjustment, generally by using expected (1995) income or reduced assets to recalculate your family contribution.

FEDERAL FAMILY EDUCATION LOANS

Stafford Loans

Formerly called Guaranteed Student Loans, the program was renamed in honor of retired Senator Robert T. Stafford (R-VT). Stafford Loans are low-interest loans to undergraduate and graduate students enrolled at least half-time. The Higher Education Amendments of 1992 made major changes in the Stafford Loan program—eligibility, loan limits, and interest rates are all different. The biggest change, however, is the opening of the program to all families without regard to financial need.

Which Stafford Loan is for You?

Students with financial need may receive a subsidized Stafford in which Uncle pays the interest while they are in school and during any deferments.

Students without financial need may receive an unsubsidized Stafford in which interest accrues while they are in school and during any deferments.

Students with partial financial need may receive a combination of the two, depending on their student status (dependent vs. independent) and level of need.

Important Note: The Supplemental Loan to Students (SLS) program has now been folded into the unsubsidized Stafford program.

Loan Limits:

Dependent Undergraduates: Freshmen may borrow up to $2,625 per year. Sophomores may borrow $3,500 per year. Juniors, seniors and fifth year undergraduates may borrow up to $5,500 per year. The maximum undergraduate loan amount is $23,000. These limits apply whether the money comes from the subsidized or unsubsidized program (or a combination of the two). For example, a freshman who receives a $1,500 subsidized Stafford may borrow a maximum of $1,125 under the unsubsidized program.

Independent Undergraduates: Freshmen may borrow $6,625 per year (at least $4,000 of which must come from the unsubsidized program). Sophomores may borrow $7,500 per year (at least $4,000 of which must come from the unsubsidized program). Juniors, seniors and fifth year undergraduates may borrow up to $10,500 per year (at least $5,000 of which must come from the unsubsidized program). The maximum amount an independent student may borrow during his or her undergraduate years is $46,000.

Graduate Students: may borrow up to $18,500 per year (at least $10,000 of which must come from the unsubsidized program) to a maximum of $138,500 ($65,500 in subsidized loans, $73,000 in unsubsidized loans). This limit includes any money they borrowed as an undergraduate.

Additional Limits: In no case may a Stafford Loan exceed the cost of attendance at your school minus any other financial aid you receive.

Prorated loan limits: Borrowing limits are prorated for programs of less than a full academic year. For example, students attending the equivalent of 1/3 of an academic year are eligible for 1/3 the maximum annual loan amount.

Loan Origination Fee and Insurance Fees. Lenders may subtract a 3% loan origination fee and a 1% insurance fee.

Interest Rate. The interest rate equals 3.1% more than the bond equivalent of the 91-day T-bill. The rate is adjusted annually. Currently, it is 7.43% and carries an 8.25% cap. Next July, the rate is supposed to drop to 2.5% above the 91-day T-bill. .

Interest Subsidy. For families with demonstrated financial need, Uncle Sam pays interest on the loan while the student is in school and for a six-month grace period after the student completes his or her studies.

Minimum Annual Repayment. $600.

Years to Repay. 5 to 10.

Who Makes Loans? Private lenders — Banks, S&Ls, Credit Unions, Insurance Companies. Also Uncle Sam (for students attending schools participating in Direct Lending).

Application Procedure. Obtain a Common Loan Application and Promissory Note from the lender. Fill out the application. Send it to your school's financial aid administrator for certification. The application then goes back to the lender and guaranteeing agency who will disburse the loan to the school. Many lenders advertise overnight processing, however, we advise you to allow two months for the paperwork flow.

Under certain circumstances, loans can be deferred, postponed, canceled or considered for forbearance.

For more information on all aspects of Staffords, see your lender or read *Loans and Grants From Uncle Sam* (inside back cover).

PLUS Loans

The Higher Education Amendments of 1992 also made major changes in the PLUS program — eligibility, loan limits, and interest rates are all different. These loans are not based on financial need so they may be used to replace your expected family contribution. In fact, creditworthy parents may borrow an unlimited amount to finance their student's college education (see Caution below).

Loan Origination Fee and Insurance Fees. Lenders may subtract a 3% loan origination fee and a 1% insurance fee.

Interest Rate. The interest rate equals 3.1% more than the bond equivalent of the 52-week T-bill. The rate is adjusted annually. Currently, it is 8.38% and carries a 9% cap (or a 10% cap for parents who took out their first loans between October 1, 1992 and July 1, 1994). There is no interest subsidy to borrowers.

Repayment begins within 60 days of taking out the loan and extends from 5 to 10 years. Repayment can be deferred while the student is in school; interest, however, keeps accruing.

Caution. The combined total of a PLUS Loan and other aid cannot exceed the student's cost of attendance.

Who Makes Loans? Private lenders—Banks, S&Ls, Credit Unions, some states, and Uncle Sam (for students attending schools participating in Direct Lending).

Application procedures are similar to Stafford Loans. Under certain conditions, loans can be deferred, postponed or canceled.

For complete information on PLUS Loans, see your lender or read *Loans and Grants From Uncle Sam.*

FEDERAL DIRECT STUDENT LOANS

Uncle Sam is convinced the student loan process would run more smoothly and at less expense by eliminating commercial lenders (and the subsidies he pays them) from the process. He proposes to make himself the lender, wiring the students' money directly to their colleges. Many people are not quite sold on the direct lending option. They point to the potential for an enormous new bureaucracy to keep tabs on the $65 billion or so in outstanding loans....a bureaucracy that will wind up costing taxpayers more than direct lending may have saved them. Also, the Department does not have the (profit) motive of the private sector; a motive that generally contributes to efficiently run, quality programs. And finally, everyone's nightmare, a direct loan program might become subject to the whims of the partisan bickering of the federal budget process. Because the response to this plan has been controversial at best, the program will be phased in slowly. About one hundred schools will participate during the pilot year (1994/95), making no more than 5% of all federal student loans. This cap will rise to 40% of all loans in 1995/96, 50% in 1996/97 and 1997/98, and 60% in 1998/99. The number of participating schools will increase accordingly. If the program is successful, these caps may be lifted beginning in 1996/97. If you're interested in direct lending, contact your financial aid office to see if your school is participating.

Are Direct Loans Different from Stafford Loans?

Not really. Uncle Sam now runs two parallel student loan programs:

Federal Family Education Loans which consists of Federal Subsidized Staffords, Federal Unsubsidized Staffords and Federal PLUS. These loans are made by commercial lenders.

Federal Direct Student Loans which consists of Federal Direct Subsidized Staffords, Federal Direct Unsubsidized Staffords, and Federal Direct PLUS. These loans are made by Uncle Sam.

Interest rates, annual and aggregate loan limits, fees, deferments, cancellations, and forbearance terms are essentially the same. Repayment options may vary slightly. The main difference, as far as the student is concerned, is with who lends them the money.

FEDERAL SUPPLEMENTAL EDUCATIONAL OPPORTUNITY GRANTS

SEOGs are administered by colleges with the $583 million in funds received from Uncle Sam each year.

Size of awards. From $100 to $4,000 per year of undergraduate study.

Criteria for Selection. Need and availability of funds. Be smart. Apply early. Priority goes to those students receiving Pell Grants.

Part-Timers. If the financial need of part-timers and independent students is at least 5% of the need of all the students at the school, then at least 5% of the SEOG funds must be set aside for support of these students.

FEDERAL WORK-STUDY

Work-Study is administered by colleges with funds received from the federal government. About $617 million per year, 713,000 participants.

Eligibility. Undergraduate and graduate students.

Criteria for Selection. Need and availability of funds. Be smart. Apply early.

Program Description. On- and off-campus employment. Salary must be at least as high as minimum wage (currently $4.25 per hour). You cannot earn more money than your award stipulates. Thus, if you receive a $1,000 award, your employment lasts until you earn $1,000 and then it is terminated for that academic year. Employment may not involve any political or religious activity nor may students be used to replace regular employees. Ten percent of the funds must be set aside for community service projects.

Part-Timers. If the financial need of less-than-full-timers and independent students is at least 5% of the need of all the students at the school, then at least 5% of the work-study funds must be set aside for support of these students.

FEDERAL PERKINS LOANS

The college acts as lender, using funds provided by the federal government. Approximately $150 million in new lending capital; over $1 billion in "revolving fund" capital (money paid back by borrowers).

Eligibility. Undergraduate and graduate students.

Part-Timers. If the financial need of less-than-full-timers and independent students is at least 5% of the need of all the students at the school, then at least 5% of the Perkins funds must be set aside for support of these students.

Criteria for Selection. Need and availability of funds. Be smart. Apply early.

Size of loan:

(1) $3,000 per year for undergraduates to a maximum of $15,000.

(2) $5,000 per year for graduate study to a maximum of $30,000 (less any Perkins money borrowed as an undergraduate).

(3) At schools participating in Uncle's *Expanded Lending Option* (to participate, schools must first have default rates under 7.5%), undergraduate students may borrow up to $4,000 per year to a maximum of $20,000; graduate students may borrow up to $6,000 per year to a maximum of $40,000 (less any Perkins money borrowed as an undergraduate).

Minimum Annual Repayment. $480

Interest rate. 5%.

Interest Subsidy. Student pays no interest while in school or during a 9-month grace period following graduation.

Repayment. 10 years.

Under certain circumstances, loans can be deferred, postponed, forgiven, or canceled. For more information on all aspects of Perkins Loans, see Loans *and Grants From Uncle Sam.*

ON DEFAULTING

Uncle Sam rewards and punishes colleges for their ability or lack thereof to collect on outstanding loans. Schools with small default rates (under 7.5%) get an increased infusion of Perkins loan capital; schools with high default rates (25% or more) may soon get zilch (and be kept from participating in any of Uncle's other loan programs). It may pay you to ask schools about their default rates before you apply.

Uncle Sam can also punish you if you are one of the defaulters. He can notify credit bureaus which will damage your credit rating. Or, he can withhold your income tax refunds until your loan is paid off (in one year alone, the IRS can collect $261 million!). As the default problem gets worse (at some trade schools, in some programs, it is as high as 85%), Uncle Sam is getting tougher, as he should. In our book, defaulters eclipse even the most parasitic protozoa!

LOAN REPAYMENT OPTIONS

Most borrowers will eventually have the choice of four different repayment plans: Standard Repayment, Extended (or Consolidated) Repayment, Graduated (or Income-Sensitive) Repayment, and Income Contingent Repayment. Standard Repayment has already been discussed.

Loan Consolidation

Students with federal loans—Stafford, Perkins, SLS, PLUS, HEAL and HPSL—who don't land a high paying job when they graduate, may want to look into loan consolidation. Under "consolidation" you can stretch repayment over a greater number of years—as many as thirty—making your monthly payments smaller but the total amount you repay much greater than under regular repayment. Married couples may consolidate their individual loans if they agree to be jointly liable for repayment even if there's a future change in their marital status.

Repayment extends for 10 years for students with less than $7,500 in loans; 12 years for students with between $7,500 and $10,000 in loans; 15 years for students with between $10,000 and $20,000; 20 years for students with between $20,000 and $40,000; 25 years for students with between $40,000 and $60,000; and 30 years for those lucky students with more than $60,000 to repay. Within these constraints, lenders must offer graduated repayment schedules (see below).

The interest rate will be the weighted average of all the loans consolidated rounded up to the nearest whole percent.

Interest Subsidies. If your consolidation loan contains only subsidized Stafford money, Uncle Sam will pay the interest on your consolidated loan during deferments. If, however, your consolidation loan contains any loans for which you were responsible for making interest payments, you will be responsible for paying all of the interest that accrues during deferment, even if your loan contains subsidized Stafford money.

For more information on consolidation, check with the institution that gave you your loan or your state guaranteeing office (addresses in *Loans and Grants from Uncle Sam*). If neither offer consolidation, contact SALLIE MAE, 1050 Thomas Jefferson Blvd. NW, Washington DC, 20007 or NELLIE MAE, Loan Consolidation Department, 50 Braintree Hill Park, Suite 300, Braintree, MA 02184.

Graduated (or Income-Sensitive) Repayment

A borrower must repay his or her entire loan within the time frame described under consolidation, however, the amount of a borrower's monthly payments increases over the life of the loan. Payments start small (when incomes are low), and increase as time goes on (presumably, while incomes also rise).

Income Contingent Repayment

The amount of your monthly payment will vary with your income. Uncle Sam is still fine tuning the details, but right now it looks like payments will range from 4% to 15% of your Adjusted Gross Income, depending on the size of your loan. Loans under $1,000 will be repaid at a rate equal to 4% of your AGI per year. Loans larger than $1,000 will be repaid at a rate equal to 4% plus .2% for each additional $1,000 borrowed (to a maximum of 15% of AGI). For example, you would repay an $11,000 loan at a rate equal to 6% of your AGI per year (4% + .2% *10). After 25 years, a borrower who has been repaying faithfully, but has not yet retired the loan, will have the rest of his or her debt forgiven. On the down-side, the IRS plans to count the amount of your loan that is forgiven as in-kind (and taxable) income. Also, students opting for this payment option might wind up paying thousands more in interest than their counterparts who choose one of the other repayment options. Finally, PLUS loans may not be repaid using the Income Contingent option.

PAUL DOUGLAS TEACHER SCHOLARSHIP PROGRAM

Uncle Sam funds 10,000 awards for HS graduates in the top 10% of their graduating class with an interest in teaching. Each state establishes its own criteria and selects recipients. The awards range up to $5,000 per year (for four years), but may not exceed financial need. Students must teach two years for every year they receive an award (one year if they teach in a shortage area). Otherwise students must repay the money. The program now operates in about 35 states.

ROBERT C. BYRD HONORS SCHOLARSHIP PROGRAM

Uncle Sam also funds an honors scholarship program. Again, each state establishes its own criteria and selects recipients (at least 10 scholars per state). The renewable awards are for $1,500 per year of academic study. They are not based on need and may be used at any US school. The program now operates in about 15 states.

NATIONAL SCIENCE SCHOLARS PROGRAM

Uncle Sam's newest state-administered program awards renewable $5,000 scholarships to HS seniors who have demonstrated outstanding academic achievement in the physical, life or computer sciences, mathematics, or engineering. Scholars are nominated by their home state; the final selection belongs to the President (in consultation with the National Science Foundation). Two awards per Congressional District.

NATIONAL SERVICE TRUST ACT

President Clinton wanted the federal government to play a larger role in fostering community-based service programs. The result was the National Service Trust Act. Volunteers will receive a minimum stipend ($7,400/year) plus health insurance, child care costs and a $4,725 education credit per year of full-time service (for a maximum of two years). The education credit can be used at any two- or four-year college, or graduate school, or be used to pay down outstanding student loans. Twenty thousand students will begin serving this year; an estimated 100,000 students will serve during the Act's three year life. Uncle Sam will provide most of the funding, but states, public agencies, and non-profit organizations will do the hiring (and the monitoring). Prime projects for funding are those that address unmet needs in education (such as assisting teachers in Head Start or in the classrooms), the environment (recycling or conservation projects), human services (building housing for the homeless, providing care to the homebound elderly, or helping in clinics that immunize young children) or public safety (teaching drug education seminars or working with community services officers within a police department).

Students who are interested in joining AmeriCorps should apply directly to a funded program, and not to the federal government. For a list of these programs, or to become part of the AmeriCorps National Service Data Bank, call the AmeriCorps hotline, 800-94-ACORPS. In Chapter 15 you'll find descriptions of some of the programs that are already up and running, as well as some addresses to help you locate eligible projects in your own community.

While the National Service Trust Act is smaller in scope than many people had hoped, its real importance is to focus attention (as well as financing) on all the local programs that have been emerging over the past decade. Studies, both formal and informal, show students who take part in community service projects achieve a heightened sense of personal and social responsibility. They have more respect for authority and more positive attitudes toward adults. And, they have enhanced self-esteem and greater self-confidence. Sen. Barbara Milkulski has been a leading advocate for national service for many years. As she says, the goals are really twofold: First, the practical goal of handling the crisis of student indebtedness; and second, a more idealistic goal of developing habits of the heart that are the foundation of this country.

THE FUTURE OF FEDERAL STUDENT AID

It's hard to predict what student aid will be like in the future. The only certainty is that money is tight and until the deficit is under control, Uncle Sam will not be getting any more generous with education dollars. *Not-So-Fun Fact:* According to the Congressional Budget Office, 13.1% of every tax dollar goes to pay the interest on our $4 trillion national debt (only defense and social security get more); a measly 3.4% of every tax dollar you pay goes to education and training!

Chapter 11
The States

All states maintain extensive programs of grants, scholarships, tuition assistance, fee reductions and loans. Last year, 1.63 million students received over $2.2 billion in need-based state aid and 231,734 shared in $255 million of non-need-based aid.

States making the most awards (over 50,000): New York, Pennsylvania, Illinois, Ohio, California, Minnesota, Michigan, New Jersey, Wisconsin and Indiana — in that order.

States spending the most (over $50 million) on student aid: New York, California, Illinois, Pennsylvania, New Jersey, Ohio, Minnesota, Michigan, Florida, North Carolina, Texas, Virginia, Washington, Georgia, Massachusetts, Indiana and Wisconsin — in that order.

States where the average award is over $1,000 — Alaska, California, Connecticut, Hawaii, Illinois, Iowa, Kansas, Louisiana, Michigan, Minnesota, Missouri, New Jersey, New Mexico, New York, North Carolina, Pennsylvania, South Carolina, Texas, Washington, and West Virginia.

ELIGIBILITY FOR STATE-BASED STUDENT AID

States determine eligibility for need-based aid in one of four ways: (1) Twenty-five states use only the federal methodology; (2) Thirteen states use the federal methodology for most of their grants and the institutional methodology (or some other hybrid methodology) for a few other programs; (3) Some states let the student's school make the decision regarding eligibility; and (4) Eleven states have their own system — Delaware, Kentucky, Louisiana, Maryland, New York, Ohio, Oklahoma, Oregon, Pennsylvania, South Carolina, and Washington.

So, how do you find out which forms to file? In almost all instances, to be considered eligible for state-based student aid, you must file Uncle Sam's FAFSA (and on it, indicate your home state). Some states, those that use the institutional methodology, might ask for the College Board's FAF (most states have their own version...be sure to ask your counselor), and finally, some states have their own applications. Important: Many states have already noted that using the federal methodology to determine eligibility means more students are qualifying for aid. Unfortunately, state grants are not entitlements, so when the money runs out, too bad! Again, apply early!

A SUMMARY OF STATE PROGRAMS

The following summary table describes current state programs other than state participation in federal programs like the Paul Douglas Teacher Scholarship, the Robert C. Byrd Honors Scholarship, National Science Scholars, the Stafford Loan and the PLUS programs. These were all discussed in Chapter 10. With regard to these last two programs, most states have a guaranteeing agency to administer loans. *Loans and Grants from Uncle Sam* gives the addresses and phone numbers of these special agencies.

Here is an explanation of the table's columns.

Column 1 — In-State Study. These are need-based grants, generally restricted to undergraduates. Most of these grants are funded with help from Uncle Sam's State Student Incentive Grant (SSIG), a program that's always on the Administration's list to cut (by both Democrats and Republicans alike), and always restored by Congress during the budget process. This year, Uncle Sam's contribution will probably go from $72 million down to $54 million, but even this smaller contribution is enough to trigger over $2 billion in state grants.

Column 2—Some Other States. These are also need-based grant programs, generally restricted to undergraduates, but these states have signed reciprocity agreements with one or more other states.

Column 3—Merit Programs. Generally, there are three kinds of merit programs. The first type is based on financial need; however, there is an academic threshold you must attain (such as a B average) to be eligible. The second program is based on academic accomplishment. But you must demonstrate financial need to qualify for a monetary award, otherwise, your recognition will be honorary. The last type of program is based solely on academic accomplishment. Your award is not affected by your financial situation. Funding for merit-based programs continues to grow much faster than funding for need-based programs (17% vs. 7% last year; 18% vs. 12% this year), as states don't want to lose their best students to other states.

Column 4—Special Loans. These loans are separate from any federal programs. For example, in Minnesota, SELF loans enable students to borrow $4,000 per year at 1.5% above the 91 day T-bill rate. For all these plans, the loan money is usually secured through tax-exempt bonds issued by the state. In some cases, out-of-state students attending a school in the state underwriting the loans may benefit from the low rates.

Column 5—Teaching. To increase the supply of teachers, many states have instituted special loan programs for students willing to become teachers, with "forgiveness" features if the students actually end up in classrooms. If the students don't go into teaching, they must repay the aid. Some programs limit their benefits to students who teach in a shortage area. This could mean a subject area like math or science. It could also mean a geographic area like rural America or the inner-city. The states listed here are those with programs in addition to the Paul Douglas Teacher Scholarship.

Column 6—Special Fields. This category covers a variety of programs designed to increase representation in other fields in which the state believes it has shortages. These fields may include medicine, nursing, special education, bilingual education, etc. Many graduate programs are included in this category.

Column 7—Minority Group Programs. The beneficiaries must usually be African-American, Latino or Native American (Eskimo, Indian, or Aleutian).

Column 8—Work-Study. State operated programs similar to the federal work-study or cooperative education programs.

Column 9—Veterans. Special state benefits to state residents who served in the Armed Forces, usually during periods of hostilities.

Column 10—National Guard. State educational benefits for serving in the state's National Guard. These are in addition to federal benefits.

Columns 11,12,13. Special benefits to state residents who are dependents of deceased or disabled veterans, or POWs, MIAs, or police/firefighters killed on duty.

Column 14—Military Dependents. These states let military personnel and their dependents stationed within the state's borders, attend in-state universities at lower in-state tuition rates.

Column 15—Tuition Savings Plans. To encourage early planning for college costs, many states allow families to purchase "Baccalaureate Bonds," the income from which is tax exempt if used to pay college expenses. A second type of savings plan is the "Prepaid Tuition Plan" in which parents can guarantee four years of tuition at any of the state's public (or in some cases, private) colleges by making a lump sum investment or periodic payments. The amount depends on the child's date of entry into college and the degree of flexibility parents desire in withdrawing funds. The state invests the money and pays the student's tuition when he or she enters college, and takes the risk of actually guaranteeing tuition. As for the tax consequences, your student will likely be liable for taxes on the fund's appreciation when he or she starts using the money—try to get a definitive ruling before you invest. While sophisticated investors can probably achieve a greater return than in either of these plans, the fact is, most families are not comfortable playing investment games. They want an easy way to guarantee they'll have enough money for their children's education, and these plans do work!

	1. In-State Study	2. Some Other States	3. Merit Programs	4. Special Loans	5. Teaching	6. Special Fields	7. Minority Gp Program	8. Work Study	9. Veterans	10. National Guard	Dependent of 11. Disabled Vet	12. POW or MIA	13. Police/Fireman	14. Active Duty	15. Tuition Savings Plan
Alabama	X				X	X	X			X	X		X	X	X
Alaska	X	X	X	X		X	X			X		X		X	X
Arizona	X				X		X			X				X	
Arkansas	X		X		X	X	X				X	X	X	X	X
California	X				X		X	X			X		X		
Colorado	X		X			X	X	X	X	X	X	X	X	X	
Connecticut	X	X	X	X			X	X	X	X	X	X		X	X
Delaware	X	X	X		X	X					X	X	X		
DC	X	X												X	
Florida	X		X			X		X			X	X		X	X
Georgia	X		X		X	X							X	X	
Guam	X			X		X								X	
Hawaii	X			X						X				X	
Idaho	X		X					X	X	X	X	X		X	
Illinois	X		X		X		X			X	X		X	X	X
Indiana	X		X				X	X							
Iowa	X		X	X				X						X	
Kansas	X		X		X	X	X	X						X	
Kentucky	X		X		X		X	X			X		X	X	X
Louisiana	X		X				X	X	X	X	X		X	X	
Maine	X	X			X	X	X			X	X	X	X	X	
Maryland	X	X	X		X	X					X	X	X	X	X
Massachusetts	X	X		X							X	X	X		
Michigan	X		X				X	X	X	X	X	X			X
Minnesota	X		X			X	X	X	X		X	X	X	X	
Mississippi	X		X		X	X	X				X	X	X	X	
Missouri	X		X		X						X		X		
Montana	X					X	X	X			X	X		X	
Nebraska	X		X			X	X	X	X	X	X	X		X	
Nevada	X			X		X	X	X	X	X	X	X	X		
New Hampshire	X	X	X	X		X					X	X		X	X
New Jersey	X		X				X		X			X	X		
New Mexico	X		X		X	X	X	X	X						
New York	X		X	X	X	X	X		X		X	X	X		
North Carolina	X		X		X	X	X	X	X	X	X	X		X	X
North Dakota	X		X		X	X				X	X	X	X	X	
Ohio	X	X	X			X					X	X	X	X	X
Oklahoma	X		X			X	X					X			X
Oregon	X					X	X						X	X	
Pennsylvania	X	X	X	X	X			X	X				X	X	
Puerto Rico	X									X					
Rhode Island	X	X	X		X	X		X							X
South Carolina	X			X		X	X				X	X	X	X	
South Dakota	X		X			X	X				X	X	X	X	
Tennessee	X		X		X		X						X	X	

	1. In-State Study	2. Some Other States	3. Merit Programs	4. Special Loans	5. Teaching	6. Special Fields	7. Minority Gp Programs	8. Work Study	9. Veterans	10. National Guard	Dependent of 11. Disabled Vet	Dependent of 12. POW or MIA	Dependent of 13. Police/Fireman	14. Active Duty	15. Tuition Savings Plan
Texas	X	X	X		X	X	X	X	X	X	X	X	X	X	
Utah	X					X								X	
Vermont	X	X		X											
Virgin Islands	X					X					X				
Virginia	X			X		X	X	X			X	X	·	X	X
Washington	X					X	X		X					X	X
West Virginia	X	X	X			X	X	X					X		
Wisconsin	X		X			X	X	X		X	X			X	
Wyoming			X			X	X			X	X			X	X

No two states have the same programs. Here are some you should ask about. Your questions might lead you to little-known or special opportunities.

Reciprocal Arrangements I. Besides the major reciprocal arrangements between states, lesser arrangements often permit students living near the state's border to study in the adjoining state at in-state tuition rates. For example, students living in Minnesota may take classes in Wisconsin, South Dakota, North Dakota, and Iowa.

Reciprocal Arrangements II. Authority to study out of state when desired course program is not offered in state. Such arrangements are often supervised by consortia such as WICHE (PO Drawer P Boulder, CO 80301) which covers most western states; the Southern Regional Education Board (592 10th Street, NW, Atlanta, GA 30318) which operates the Academic Common Market in the southern states; and the New England Regional Student Program administered by the New England Board of Education (45 Temple Place, Boston, MA 02111). The Midwest Student Exchange Program of the Midwestern Higher Education Exchange began in 1994/95.

Reciprocal Arrangements III. WICHE has introduced an even larger reciprocal study program in which students may pay reduced tuition at any of the 55 state schools in the region. The reduced rate equals resident tuition plus 50%; a large savings over regular non-resident rates.

Tuition Equalization. These programs reduce the difference in tuition costs between in state public and private colleges. Examples: Alabama, Florida, Georgia, Kansas, Kentucky, New Mexico, North Carolina, Ohio, Vermont and Virginia. Last year, these states made grants worth well over $107 million.

Grant Programs I. Most states provide special assistance to students attending private colleges in state. Such awards are need based.

Grant Programs II. Some states provide need-based assistance to residents attending schools out-of-state. Examples: Alaska, Delaware, Maine, Maryland, Massachusetts, New Hampshire, Ohio, Pennsylvania, Rhode Island, Vermont, West Virginia, and Wisconsin. These states made 22,638 grants last year, worth $14.5 million.

Free Scholarship Search. Alabama, Florida, Maine and Vermont offer state residents (free) individualized lists of potential financial aid sources.

Discounts for Senior Citizens. Alabama, Colorado, Connecticut, Kentucky, Maine, Minnesota, Nebraska, New Mexico, South Carolina, Vermont, and Wyoming all give tuition discounts to seniors. Some states waive tuition entirely. Eligibility varies from state to state, but generally, students must be state residents aged 60+ and attend state schools. Sometimes the discount is given to students only on a space available basis.

Community College Partnerships. Many states are creating partnerships between two- and four-year colleges to help make the transition seamless. Sometimes students are guaranteed admission to the four-year school. Sometimes they're offered additional aid opportunities (and sometimes they are just given guidance on course selection). For example, Colorado, Florida, Illinois, Kansas, Maryland, Massachusetts, Minnesota, New Mexico, North Carolina, Ohio, West Virginia and Wyoming.

Community Service Opportunities. Many states were way ahead of the community service bandwagon. Some are tied in to AmeriCorps—Colorado, Kentucky, Maryland, Minnesota, and Vermont; others are funding their own—Connecticut, Georgia, Illinois, Iowa, Kansas, Missouri, and North Carolina.

INNOVATIVE STATE PROGRAMS

Be on the lookout for these. There is a lot of action on the state level—some of which will result in important new programs (and some which will be allowed to fizzle).

New York: Liberty Scholarships would pay the non-tuition costs of low income families who attend school in New York. Liberty Partnerships would provide them with counseling and tutoring. This program may finally get funded for 1995.

Georgia: Helping Outstanding Pupils Educationally (HOPE) will ensure that every qualified (3.0 GPA or better) graduate of a GA high school with a family income under $100,000 will receive a grant to cover 45 credit hours (in-state tuition, fees and books) at any GA public school. State residents attending tech schools or private colleges in Georgia qualify for some assistance as well. The program is funded by the Lottery for Education. For more information (in Georgia), call 800-546-HOPE.

Michigan: Tuition Incentive Program (TIP). Low income students can get free tuition at community colleges. Those who complete community college are eligible for a $2,000 voucher for use at any of Michigan's four year colleges.

Illinois: College Savings Bonds. Illinois was the first state to encourage families to save for college expenses via tax-exempt (non-callable) zero coupon bonds. In Illinois, bond holders can also receive a Bonus Incentive Grant (BIG).

Vermont. Vermont Value Loan Program reduces the principal balance on the Stafford and PLUS by 1% during each year of repayment.

Arkansas, Louisiana, Indiana, and Virginia: In Arkansas, they're called Academic Challenge Scholarships. In Indiana, they're called Twenty-First Century Scholars. They all have similar themes: States guarantee to pay in-state tuition for low-income students who make certain commitments. For example, the student must maintain a specified GPA in college prep courses and remain drug free. This performance-based tuition waiver for at-risk students has been nicknamed "The Taylor Plan" after Patrick Taylor, a Louisiana oil man who realized that many people drop out of HS because they perceive it as a dead end. He figured if you promised at-risk students a college education (assuming they stayed out of trouble and met the admission standards), you'd see a drastic increase in levels of educational achievement.

Maine. Maine residents attending out-of-state schools, and out-of-state students attending Maine schools can take out a "Super Loan" at 1% below the current Stafford rate. The program is available through 39 participating lenders.

Virginia and Texas: Special incentive grants to induce students of one racial group to attend a state public university in which another racial group makes up a significant proportion of the student body.

Colorado, Florida and Minnesota: Colorado's Postsecondary Options Plan, Florida's Dual Enrollment Plan and Minnesota's Postsecondary Enrollment Options Act allow public HS students to take courses at no charge at any college in the state that will admit them (the Florida program is restricted to state schools). Students receive both high school and college credit for their work.

Directory of State Agencies

Alabama
205-281-1921
AL Commission on Higher Education
3465 Norman Bridge Road
Montgomery, AL 36105-2310

Alaska
907-465-2854
Commission on Postsecondary Ed.
3030 Vintage Blvd.
Juneau, AK 99801

Arizona
602-229-2593
Commission for Postsecondary Ed.
2020 N. Central Avenue, #275
Phoenix, AZ 85004

Arkansas
501-324-9300
Department of Higher Education
114 E. Capitol St.
Little Rock, AR 72201

California
916-445-0880
CA Postsecondary Ed. Commission
1303 J. Street, #500
Sacramento, CA 95814

Colorado
303-866-2723
Commission on Higher Education
1300 Broadway, 2nd Floor
Denver, CO 80203

Connecticut
203-566-2618
Department of Higher Education
61 Woodland Street
Hartford, CT 06105

Delaware
302-577-3240
Higher Education Commission
820 N. French Street
Wilmington, DE 19801

District of Columbia
202-727-3685
DC Office of Postsecondary Education
2100 Martin Luther King Jr. Ave., SE
Washington, DC 20020

Florida
904-488-4095
Office of Student Financial Assistance
Department of Education
1344 Florida Education Center
Tallahassee, FL 32399

Georgia
404-414-3000
Georgia Student Finance Authority
2082 East Exchange Place, #200
Tucker, GA 30084

Hawaii
808-948-8213
Postsecondary Ed Commission
Bachman Hall, Room 209
2444 Dole Street
Honolulu, HI 96822

Idaho
208-334-2270
State Board of Education
650 West State Street
Boise, ID 83720

Illinois
217-782-3442
IL State Board of Higher Education
#4 West Old Capitol Plaza
Springfield, IL 62701

Indiana
317-232-2350
State Student Assistance Comm.
150 West Market St., 5th floor
Indianapolis, IN 46204

Iowa
515-242-6703
Iowa College Aid Commission
914 Grand Ave., #201
Des Moines, IA 50309

Kansas
913-296-3517
Board of Regents, State of Kansas
Suite 609, Capitol Tower
400 SW 8th Street
Topeka, KS 66603

Kentucky
502-564-7990
Higher Ed. Assistance Authority
1050 US 127 South, Suite 102
West Frankfort Office Complex
Frankfort, KY 40601-4323

Louisiana
504-922-1011
Student Financial Assistance Comm.
PO Box 91202
Baton Rouge, LA 70821-9202

Maine
207-287-2183
Maine Ed. Assistance Division
State House Station, #119
One Weston Court
Augusta, ME 04330

Maryland
410-974-5370
MD Higher Ed. Commission
State Scholarship Administration
16 Francis Street
Annapolis, MD 21401

Massachusetts
617-727-9420
Higher Ed. Coordinating Council
Room 1401, McCormack Bldg.
One Ashton Place
Boston, MA 02108

Michigan
517-373-3394
Higher Ed Assistance Authority
PO Box 30008
Lansing, MI 48909

Minnesota
612-296-3974
Higher Ed. Coordinating Board
Capitol Square Building, #400
550 Cedar Street
St. Paul, MN 55101

Mississippi
601-982-6570
Board of Trustees of State
  Institutions of Higher Learning
Student Financial Aid
3825 Ridgewood Road
Jackson, MS 39211-6453

Missouri
314-751-2361
Coordinating Board for Higher Ed.
3515 Amazonas Drive
Jefferson City, MO 65109

Montana
406-444-6594
Board of Regents for Higher Education
2500 Broadway
Helena, MT 59620

Nebraska
Contact Individual Schools Directly

Nevada
702-687-5915
State Department of Education
400 West King Street
Capitol Complex
Carson City, NV 89710

New Hampshire
603-271-2555
Postsecondary Ed. Commission
2 Industrial Park Drive
Concord, NH 03301-8512

New Jersey
609-588-3268, 800-792-8670
Higher Education Commission
Office of Student Assistance
4 Quakerbridge Plaza, CN 540
Trenton, NJ 08625

New Mexico
505-827-7383
Commission on Higher Education
1068 Cerrillos Road
Santa Fe, NM 87501

New York
518-473-0431
Higher Ed. Services Commission
One Commerce Plaza
Albany, NY 12255

North Carolina
919-549-8614
State Ed. Assistance Authority
PO Box 2688
Chapel Hill, NC 27515

North Dakota
701-224-4114
ND State Board of Higher Ed.
Student Assistance Program
600 East Boulevard
Bismark, ND 58505

Ohio
614-466-7420
OH Student Aid Commission
PO Box 182452
Columbus, OH 43218-2452

Oklahoma
405-522-4356
Oklahoma State Regents for
  Higher Ed
500 Education Building
State Capitol Complex
Oklahoma City, OK 73105

Oregon
503-687-7385
State Scholarship Commission
1500 Valley River Drive, #100
Eugene, OR 97401

Pennsylvania
717-257-2800, (PA) 800-692-7435
Higher Education Assistance Agency
Town House, 660 Boas Street
Harrisburg, PA 17102

Rhode Island
401-277-2050
Higher Education Assistance Authority
560 Jefferson Boulevard
Warwick, RI 02886

South Carolina
803-737-2265
SC Commission on Higher Education
1333 Main Street, #200
Columbia, SC 29201

South Dakota
605-773-3134
Office of the Secretary
Department of Education and
  Cultural Affairs
700 Governors Drive
Pierre, SD 57501-2291

Tennessee
615-741-1346, TN 800-342-1663
TN Student Assistance Corporation
404 James Robertson Parkway
Parkway Towers, Suite 1950
Nashville, TN 37243-0820

Texas
512-483-6331
Higher Education Coordinating Board
Box 12788, Capitol Station
Austin, TX 78711

Utah
801-538-5247
Utah State Board of Regents
335 W.N. Temple, 3 Triad, Suite 550
Salt Lake City, UT 84180-1205

Vermont
802-655-9602
Vermont Student Assistance Corp.
Champlain Mill, Box 2000
Winooski, VT 05404

Virginia
804-225-2623
Council of Higher Education
James Monroe Building
101 North 14th Street
Richmond, VA 23219

Washington
206-586-6404
Higher Education Coordinating Board
917 Lake Ridge Way, GV-11
Olympia, WA 98504

West Virginia
304-347-1211
Higher Education Grant Program
PO Box 4007
Charleston, WV 25364

Wisconsin
608-267-2206
State of Wisconsin Higher
  Educational Aids Board
PO Box 7885
Madison, WI 53707

Wyoming
307-766-2116
University of Wyoming
Student Financial Aid
Box 3335, University Station
Laramie, WY 82071-3335

Guam
617-734-2921, x3657
Financial Aid Office
University of Guam
Mangilao, Guam 96923

Puerto Rico
809-758-3350
Council on Higher Education
Box 23305, UPR Station
Rio Piedras, PR 00931

Virgin Islands
809-774-4546
Board of Education
Commandant Gade, OV #11
St. Thomas, VI 00801

Part V

The Big Alternatives

Ok. You are willing to pick up a little maturity along with your education. You are willing to invest some extra time into earning a baccalaureate. And you want to start your professional career without the staggering burden of student debt. What can you do? You can investigate two major alternative methods of financing an education: (1) Letting the boss pay for it or (2) letting the military pay for it.

Part V covers both of these "employee" tuition plans—those found in Madison Avenue corporate offices and those sponsored by the US Military. You can pick up nearly $3 billion along these routes.

Chapter 12
Letting the Boss Pay for It

COMPANY TUITION AID

A little history.

Until 1984, you could go to work for a company that had a tuition reimbursement plan (and about 20 million employees were covered by such plans), take college courses on your own time, and let the employer foot the bill.

The Deficit Reduction Act of 1984 changed all this. It ruled that courses had to be job-related to qualify as a benefit. Courses not job-related, but paid for by the employer, had to be declared as taxable income.

That ruling pulled the rug out from what had promised to become a major alternative program for young people. The reason: Jobs at the bottom are usually so narrowly defined that few of the many educational explorations required for a degree could pass the "job-related test." Why would a shipping clerk need a course in American History?

While hurting people at the entry level, the law had little impact on the educational pursuits of the higher-ups. A manager might justify a course in English Literature to improve her writing skills and a sales manager could qualify for an Anthropology program to better understand the cultural factors that influence buying.

The Tax-Reform Act of 1986 brought back the exclusion of non job-related tuition benefits (Section 127 for anyone who cares to read the tax code), but limited the exclusion to $5,250. Since then, Congress has continued to extend the exclusion, but on a year-to-year basis. The exclusion expires every September 30, however, with nearly 3,000 employers offering Section 127 plans, we anticipate another extension this year.

Graduate students, as well as undergrads, are eligible for this exclusion!

Reimbursements for courses that are job-related remain 100% tax excludable for both undergraduate and graduate students (with no dollar ceiling).

Even if your employer does reimburse you for tuition, and the reimbursement remains a tax-free benefit, there may be some strings attached. For example, you may have to stay with the firm for a set number of years after you graduate, or maintain a certain grade point average while in school. These requirements are only fair—after all, employers help employees with their education for the good of the company, not just for the good of the employee. Ford is one company that realizes this; it pays 100% of any course approved by a boss.

Still, a better program for the beginner is Cooperative Education.

COOPERATIVE EDUCATION

Cooperative Education is a program which combines formal studies with an off-campus job related to your major. The money earned on the job will, in most cases, cover college costs. In some schools, practically the entire student body participates in cooperative education. Examples: Northeastern University (MA), and GMI Engineering & Management Institute (MI). There are three common methods for rotating between school and work:

- **The alternating method.** Under this method, you are a full-time student for a term or semester, then you work for a term or a semester, with the cycle repeating itself until you graduate—usually in five years.

- **The parallel method.** Here you attend classes part time and work between 15 and 25 hours a week. You may be a student in the morning and a worker in the afternoon, or vice versa. This method, too, may require five years for degree completion.
- **Extended day method.** The student works full-time and attends school in the evening.

Employers like the co-op program, considering it, in the Wall Street Journal's words, "a source of realistic, work-oriented, future full-time employees."

Some statistics about cooperative education: 900 participating colleges, 50,000 participating employers, 200,000 enrolled students who earn $1.3 billion each year. The biggest employer, offering the widest choice of work sites, academic plans and career fields: Uncle Sam (over 18,000 students).

More information on cooperative education:

1. *A College Guide to Cooperative Education* from the National Commission for Cooperative Education, 360 Huntington Avenue, Boston, MA 02115. For both grad students and undergrads.
2. *Earn and Learn* from Octameron will link you up with Uncle Sam's cooperative education program — the directory contains an overview of 18,000 federal coop positions, the 50 sponsoring agencies, the career fields and the location of work sites (see inside back cover).
3. *Your Home State.* Nearly half the states have work-study or coop programs. If your high school counselor doesn't have the address of your home state's Cooperative Education Center, call your state agency (listed in Chapter 11) and ask them for the information.

JUNIOR FELLOWSHIPS

This is another program from Uncle Sam; 5,000 openings for good students with financial need. Junior Fellowships provide opportunities to work in a federal agency during all academic calendar breaks — winter, spring, summer. There is no restriction on college choice. Students can put together as much as $12,500 in earnings over four years. Often, a professional position with Uncle is available following graduation.

The program is poorly advertised. In consequence, it has never been filled to authorized levels. Last year, for example, the program had nearly 3,900 vacancies. Application and selection are made in the senior year in high school.

For more information on Junior Fellowships, get *Earn and Learn,* as described above.

INTERNSHIPS

It's hard to draw the line between cooperative education and internships. Two general distinctions: The alternating involvement between formal studies and work, in cooperative education, extends throughout a student's college career, while internships often last only one semester or one summer break. Participants in cooperative education always get a paycheck; interns may or may not. In fact, the more "desirable" the internship, the less the pay. Those that do pay generally offer students from $75 to $100 per week.

More information on internships:

The National Directory of Internships ($22) from the National Society for Internships and Experiential Education, 122 St. Mary's St., Raleigh, NC 27605, 919/787-3263.

Chapter 13
Putting on the Uniform

Don't overlook the military as a source of financial aid. You can pick up tuition dollars before you enter the service, while in uniform, and after being discharged.

There are programs for active duty personnel and programs for being in the Reserves or the National Guard. And there are programs for officers and programs for enlisted people. .

Military tuition benefits are dispensed with no reference to financial need. You qualify for them, whether you are rich or poor. But they are not free. The military will want something in return. As a minimum it will require you to get a haircut, salute superior officers and give a few years of your time.

Service Status	Typical Programs
Before Entering Service	Military Academies ROTC Medical Programs One-Shot Programs
In Service	Off-Duty Programs Commissioned Officers Formal Programs Leading to Associate, Baccalaureate, Graduate Degrees
After Service	Montgomery GI Bill Veterans Educational Assistance Program (VEAP) Dependent Benefits

BEFORE ENTERING SERVICE

Military Academies

The academies are extremely competitive. Good grades, extracurricular activities, leadership and athletic excellence are in demand. So are superb health and solid SAT scores. On the math portion you should have 600+ and your combined score should be 1200 or more. Contact the academies during your junior year of high school. Most appointments are made by Representatives and Senators. Tell your elected officials about your interest. Make sure they open a file on you in their offices. Keep feeding that file with your achievements. Also add recommendations. Make sure you obtain recommendations from people who are deemed important by the elected officials.

ROTC Scholarships

The military has one-year, two-year, and four-year ROTC scholarships. These scholarships will pay for tuition, books and fees. You will also get a $100 monthly allowance or a flat stipend (e.g., $1,000 per year). Note: The Army now limits its ROTC awards to 80% of tuition, or $8,000, whichever is greater. Some schools offer free room and board to ROTC scholarship winners, but room, board, transportation and miscellaneous expenses are generally your responsibility. A 1200 SAT with 600+ on the math portion will enhance your chances for an ROTC scholarship. So will a varsity letter and membership in the National Honor Society. Application here, too, should be made during your junior year of high school. There will be an interview. Before the interview, brush up on current affairs. Also, be prepared to give your reasons for seeking a military career. An interest in a science or engineering major will enhance your chances of winning an ROTC scholarship. ROTC is not offered at all colleges. The services will provide you with a list. You have to select a college from that list and secure admission yourself.

The Regular ROTC Program

This is not a scholarship program. Students join the program in their freshman year, at colleges that offer ROTC. For two years they march and salute for free. In their junior and senior years, participants do get paid: $100 per month.

ROTC-Coop Education Combination

The Army reserves cooperative education positions for some ROTC cadets in nearby Army installations. These positions, which provide added earnings, will also lead to federal employment after the participant has served on active duty.

Military Medical Programs

See Chapter 20

One-Shot Programs

On occasion, the Navy and the Air Force need highly specialized technical people and will use financial aid as a recruiting tool. For instance, the Air Force has a "College Senior Engineer Program" for students in electrical, nuclear, astronautical and aeronautical engineering. Students can sign up during their junior year. In their senior year, they will receive $1740 or $900 per month. After graduation, they are called to active duty, attend Officer Training School and serve as a commissioned officer.

MORE INFORMATION

Academies:

Admissions Office, USMA
606 Thayer Road
West Point, NY 10996

Director of Cadet Admissions
USAF Academy
Colorado Springs, CO 80840

Candidate Guidance
US Naval Academy
Leahy Hall
Annapolis, MD 21402

Admissions
US Merchant Marine Academy
Kings Point, NY 11024

Admissions
US Coast Guard Academy
15 Mohegan Avenue
New London, CT 06320

ROTC:

Army ROTC
800-USA-ROTC

Marine Corps
800-NAV-ROTC

Navy ROTC
800-NAV-ROTC

Air Force ROTC
800-423-USAF

IN SERVICE EDUCATIONAL BENEFITS

Commissioned Officer

Each year, the services select hundreds of officers to attend graduate schools. The chosen officers receive full pay and allowances and have all their educational expenses met while pursuing their master's degree or doctorate.

Off-Duty Programs

All services have arrangements with civilian colleges and not only permit but encourage off-duty course work, with the services paying up to 90% of the tuition costs (amount varies with rank and length of service). Through credit transfers and arrangements with accrediting institutions, such off-duty courses can be accumulated to gain credit for associate, baccalaureate or even master's degrees. For more information on this Concurrent Admissions Program (CoAP) contact Servicemembers Opportunity Colleges, One Dupont Circle, Suite 700, Washington DC 20036.

Concurrent Bonuses and Benefits

Through the National Guard and Army Reserves, you can receive approximately $6,120 in education benefits under the Montgomery GI Bill. You can also earn cash bonuses—for example $1,500-$2,000 for enlistment in the reserves; up to $2,000 for completing advanced training in the National Guard. The Army Reserve, National Guard, and the Regular Army also offer repayment on federal student loans as an incentive for enlistment in selected skills. In the Army Reserve and National Guard, you may have up to $10,000 forgiven (Stafford, Perkins and SLS). Forgiveness comes at the rate of 15% or $500 per year, whichever is greater (to a maximum of $1,500 per year). In the Regular Army, repayment is 33% of the loan or $1,500, whichever is greater (to a maximum of $10,000), for each year of active service. Contact your recruiting officer for more details.

AFTER SERVICE BENEFITS

The Montgomery GI Bill

Congress enacted a new GI Bill which affects everyone enlisting after July 1, 1985 (the program has 400,000 participants to date). It is a contributory system. The soldier or sailor or airman, while on active duty, allocates $100 per month (to a maximum of $1,200) to an educational fund. At the end of a four-year enlistment, the Veteran's Administration provides the participant with up to $400 per month for 36 months to supplement his or her educational costs. The Army sweetens the pot with education bonuses for enlisting in what it calls critical "Military Occupation Specialties" (MOS). This could add up to $18,000 (for a four year enlistment) to the $14,400 already earned. The Army calls this bonus "The New Army College Incentive." Call 1-800-USA-ARMY for more information.

The Veteran's Educational Assistance Program

For those of you who enlisted before July 1, 1985, don't worry. The military has education benefits for you, too. In fact, you will find the military educational incentives to be similar. VEAP is also a contributory system. The participant can pledge up to $2,700, either in monthly installments or as a lump sum. The government will match the contribution 2 for 1, up to $5,400. At the end of your enlistment you have as much as $8,100 for tuition money. As additional incentive, the Army College Fund will add up to $18,300 (for a four year enlistment) if you sign up for a critical MOS. If you are eligible for these benefits, take advantage of them soon. VEAP is likely to be phased out sometime in the near future.

Dependents Education Assistance

Wives and children of veterans who died or were totally disabled as the result of service qualify for Veterans Administration educational benefits. These benefits are also extended to dependents of former Prisoners of War and soldiers classified as MIA—Missing in Action.

State Educational Benefits

Most states have aid programs for Veterans and their dependents. See Chapter 11 and write to your state's Office of Veteran Affairs (addresses in *Need A Lift*, PO Box 1050, Indianapolis, IN 46206, $2.00).

BENEFITS FOR MILITARY DEPENDENTS

Army

1. Army Emergency Relief. Scholarships for unmarried children of active duty, retired, disabled or deceased soldiers. For scholarships, apply by March 1 to Army Emergency Relief, 200 Stovall Street, Alexandria, VA 22314.
2. Summary of Educational Benefits. Request DA Pamphlet 352-2, Headquarters, Department of the Army DAAG-EDD, Washington, D. C. 20314.

Air Force

Air Force Aid Society. Grant program ($1,000) for children of active duty, Title 10 Reservists, retired or deceased Air Force members. Air Force Aid Society, Education Assistance Department, 1745 Jefferson Davis Highway, Suite 202, Arlington, VA 22202-3410. March deadlines.

Navy/Marines

Dependent's Scholarship Program for U.S. Navy, Marine Corps, and Coast Guard Dependents. More than 75 Navy-oriented organizations currently sponsor scholarships or offer aid for study beyond the high school level. Dependent sons and daughters of Navy, Marine Corps, Coast Guard, and former members are eligible for these scholarships or aid. Information may be obtained by getting *Need A Lift?* (see below).

ASSOCIATION BENEFITS FOR THE FAMILIES OF FORMER MILITARY

Former military families tend to congregate in organizations after leaving the service. Nearly every military association sponsors student aid programs to the children of its members. For a comprehensive list, obtain the useful annual book *Need a Lift?* published by The American Legion, Emblem Sales, PO Box 1050, Indianapolis, IN 46206. Cost: **$3.00, prepaid.** Here are a few examples:

AMVETS Memorial Scholarship

$1,000/year scholarships for 4 years. Veterans, HS seniors (who are sons or daughters of veterans), Must demonstrate need and academic achievement and be a US citizen. Forms available after January 1. AMVETS National Headquarters, attn. Scholarships, 4647 Forbes Blvd., Lanham, MD 20706.

Reserve Officer Association

Henry J. Reilly Memorial Scholarships. 75 awards for dependents of Association members. Deadlines fluctuate between April 1 and April 30. Scholarship Fund, ROA, 1 Constitution Avenue, N.E., Washington, DC 20002.

Retired Officers Scholarship Program

Not a grant, but an interest-free loan program. Maximum: $8,000 ($2,000/yr.) spread over five years, for unmarried dependent children of active and retired commissioned members of the military. Coast Guard, NOAA and Public Health Service. Apply to Administrator, Scholarship Committee, TROA, 201 N. Washington St., Alexandria, VA 22314.

SCAMP

Scholarships for Children of American Military Personnel (SCAMP) Awards for children of armed service personnel who served in Vietnam and were killed in action, missing in action, or prisoners of war. Also eligible are children of those men and women who gave their lives to the great challenge of Space, and eligible children of Desert Storm armed forces personnel. $3,500-$5,000. By July 31. SCAMP Grants, 136 S. Fuller Ave., Los Angeles, CA 90036.

A POSSIBLE STRATEGY

Go on active duty for three or four years. While on active duty, take off-duty courses (for which the military will pay up to 90% of the tuition costs) and make sure the courses add up to an associate degree. At the same time participate in the Montgomery GI Bill. When you are ready for discharge, you will have credit for two years of college and a tuition kitty of at least $9000 (more if you were in the infantry) to help you pay for the last two years of college. By the time you get your degree, you will be one, or at the most, two years older than your contemporaries who did not go into service. That minor disadvantage will be offset by somewhat greater maturity and self-confidence. And you'll probably be free of debt.

Part VI
Special Opportunities

Chapter 14
Private Sources with Few Strings

COCA COLA SCHOLARS FOUNDATION, INC.
150 scholarships per year, 50 for $5,000/year, renewable for up to 4 years at the college of one's choice. 100 are $1,000 per year, renewable for up to 4 years. Applicants must be high school seniors. Applications available only through senior's high school guidance office. First application must be postmarked on or before October 31. Course of study in any discipline. Merit-based scholarship emphasizing leadership. Write to Coca-Cola Scholars Foundation, PO Box 442, Atlanta, GA 30301, (404) 733-5420.

ELKS NATIONAL FOUNDATION
Nearly 500 awards, over $2 million awarded. HS senior, US citizen. Scholarship, leadership, and financial need. Application from local Elk Lodge. By mid-January.

HATTIE M. STRONG FOUNDATION
Interest-free loans for college students within one year of graduation. Up to $2,500/year. Repayment based on monthly earnings. Applications available between January 1 and March 31 for consideration for the scholastic year beginning the following September. Hattie M. Strong Foundation, 1735 Eye St., NW, Suite 705, Washington, DC 20006.

HITACHI FOUNDATION
The Yoshiyama Award. Given annually to 6-8 high school seniors. Not a scholarship and not based on academic achievements. Students may not nominate themselves. Award is accompanied by a gift of $5,000 over two years with no restrictions as to how gift is to be used. Award is in recognition of outstanding community service by high school students. Nominees need not be college-bound. No later than April 1. Nominations to Yoshiyama Award, PO Box 19247, Washington, DC 20036. (202) 457-0588.

PICKETT & HATCHER EDUCATIONAL FUND, INC.
Low interest loan program. Residents of Southeastern United States, US Citizen. Preference in areas other than law, medicine, or ministry. Has helped 19,000 students since 1938. Scholastic ability, character, financial need. Request application blanks from Pickett & Hatcher Educational Fund, P.O. Box 8169, Columbus, GA 31908.

SCHOLARSHIP FOUNDATION OF AMERICA
Scholarship competition for students who have demonstrated outstanding academic achievement (and have SATs of at least 1200) or who excel in the performing or visual arts. $1,000-$5,000. No deadline. Scholarship Foundation of America, 55 Highway 35, Suite 5, Red Bank, NJ 07701. Must pay $5 application fee.

Chapter 15
Money in Your Community

Just about every community offers scholarship assistance to its young citizens. The grants can vary in size from one hundred dollars to several thousand. Community awards are usually circumscribed in their geographic coverage and there is no central registry for these kinds of opportunities. You must learn about them yourself. Read the local newspaper carefully, especially the page devoted to club and community affairs. Visit the Chamber of Commerce. It might keep track of business and corporate scholarships offered in your area. Also visit the American Legion Post. The legionnaires take a special interest in helping people with their education. And finally, ask your high school counselor! Here are some examples:

Single State

Examples: the *MESA* program in California; *The New Hampshire Charitable Fund/ Student Aid Program*; the *Piper Scholars* program in Texas.

A County

Example: *The Blandin Foundation's* awards in Itasca County, Hill City and Remer school districts.

Your City

Examples: Students attending public school in Cleveland (grades 7-12) accumulate scholarship money for good grades; $40 for each A, $20 for each B, $10 for each C and a $10 bonus for taking "core" courses. In its first four years, the nearly 3,500 participants earned about $1 million for college tuition. Similar programs have now been started in Wellington, OH and Englewood, NJ. To learn more about starting this program in your city (or high school), write, *Scholarships in Escrow*, Cleveland Initiative for Education, 2000 E. Ninth Street, #825, Cleveland, OH 44115.

Your Community

Look for scholarship bulletins from civic associations, businesses, PTA chapters, social and professional clubs, fraternal organizations, patriotic and veterans organizations. Some communities do very well by their students. For example, the journalist Carl Rowan has founded a program called "Project Excellence" that awards over $250,000 per year to graduating seniors in the Washington DC area. In addition to private donors in your community, you should look toward larger local foundations. There are nearly 400 community funds nationwide, with assets totaling more than $6 billion. From this money, these foundations award nearly $100 million to education projects annually!

Your High School

Many high schools have established information clearing houses to work in conjunction with the guidance office. Students (and their parents) may attend workshops on college financing; they receive individual assistance on filing aid applications; they have access to current financial aid literature; and in some instances, they can tap into computerized scholarship data bases. ALL FOR FREE! Some schools have even created foundations to provide "last dollar scholarships" for students with exceptional financial need. Examples: The Scholarship Fund of Alexandria (VA), I Know I Can, Columbus (OH), CollegeBound Foundation, Baltimore (MD) and California Community Foundation, Los Angeles (CA). **The Renaissance Education Foundation** is another growing example. Funded by local businesses, nearly 3,500 "Renaissance Schools" nationwide offer students rewards for their academic performance. These rewards range from discounts at local stores (for students receiving A's, B's and C's) to $50 dollar savings bonds and college tuition credits (for students with all A's). While not a scholarship program per se, it is a program that's improving test scores, grade point averages, and attendance at schools across the country. For information about setting up this student-incentive program, write the *Renaissance Education Foundation*, 7801 E. Bus Lake Road, Suite 100, Minneapolis, MN 55439, or call 800-624-5534.

I Have A Dream

Over a decade ago, the very wealthy Eugene Lang promised college scholarships (and extra counseling/tutoring) to an entire sixth grade class at his former elementary school in East Harlem. In 1986, he created the I Have A Dream Foundation to assist other people in starting similar projects. He has become a hero. Today, about 10,000 students benefit from over 140 "I Have A Dream" projects in 41 cities across the country. Unfortunately, needy students can't apply directly for this assistance; they can only hope someone will adopt their class (and at a minimum investment of $300,000/class, benefactors are hard to find). It's still too early to tell whether the program has been effective, but corporate America is jumping on the bandwagon...witness "The Pepsi Challenge" in which the soft-drink company provides up to $2,000 in college scholar-ship money for "at-risk" students at selected high schools in Detroit and Dallas who meet certain GPA and attendance requirements.

Dollars for Scholars

Dollars for Scholars chapters are community-wide, volunteer-operated scholarship foundations affiliated with the *Citizen's Scholarship Foundation of America, Inc.* (CSFA) A local board of trustees organizes and publicizes its program in the community, then goes on to raise local funds for distribution to local students. CSFA provides nonprofit status, guides, and materials for chapter operations. All funds raised locally are distributed by a local awards committee. Ask your counselor if your community has a Dollars for Scholars chapter. If not, and you'd like to start one, write: Volunteer Services Coordinator, PO Box 297, St. Peter, MN 56082, or call (507) 931-1682.

Community Service Programs

While the Corporation for National and Community Service will fund about 20,000 AmeriCorps positions this year (see Chapter 10), there are even more opportunities available via your home state or a local agency. These 80+ state and local organizations spend over $131 million annually on conservation and youth-service corps and enable 30,000 additional volunteers to be rewarded for work on projects like education, the environment and public safety. While each community is free to run its own program, there are several common threads. In general, corps members work on projects in teams made up of 5-10 people from diverse backgrounds (this racial, ethnic, and economic diversity is at the heart of most programs — everyone benefits from the experiences of one another). In exchange for service, they receive a living allowance (ranging from $100 to $170 per week) and a bonus upon completion of their service commitment. Bonuses range from $1,000 to $5,000 per year of full-time service to a maximum of $10,000. Some programs don't require you to use the bonus for education expenses; others just give smaller bonuses to the non-college bound. In general, the higher the weekly stipend, the lower the education bonus. Also, in most programs, workers wear an easily identifiable uniform (for example, red t-shirts).

Here are some sample programs:

City Volunteer Corps (New York City). Founded in 1984, this was one of the country's first community-based service programs. Around 750 volunteers each year log in countless hours helping the elderly, tutoring children and cleaning up parks. In addition, volunteers who have dropped out of high school are required to complete work for their GED.

Los Angeles Youth Corps. In Los Angeles, volunteers are leading efforts to rebuild burned out buildings, plant community gardens in vacant lots, and restore areas affected by rioting.

City Year (Boston). City Year is frequently mentioned as a model for a national plan. The nearly 500 participants (ages 17-24) meet every morning for calisthenics before they fan out to start their work—cleaning parks, organizing summer camps, leading day trips, etc. Workers earn $100 per week with a $5,000 bonus at the end of 9-months (the money need not be used for college). Workers are docked for missed days. Before the year is over, workers must register to vote, obtain a library card, produce a resume, learn to prepare their taxes, and get their GED (if not already a high school graduate).

Civic Works (Baltimore). Civic Works is shorter in duration, only six months long. Participants take classes in carpentry, construction, household management and job readiness, then use these skills to revitalize low-income areas.

Volunteer Maryland places more emphasis on part-time volunteer efforts. Participants are striving to link thousands of Marylanders (who are not part of the program) with their local volunteer organizations.

Georgia Peach Corps. The Peach Corps employs about 100 youths, ages 17-25. They work at minimum wage on selected human service and public works projects in rural communities. At the end of one year, they receive $5,000 in credit toward tuition costs at any college nationwide.

Delta Service Corps. Administered by the Arkansas Division on Volunteerism, the Delta Service Corps places workers age 17+ in existing community organizations across some of the poorest regions of our country (142 counties in Arkansas, Louisiana and Mississippi). Corps members receive a $5,000 education voucher for each of two years of full-time service; $2,000 for each of three years if they're only serving part-time. In January, 1993, the Corps began training its first 270 workers (it soon plans to expand to 1,000).

Amerasian Service Team (Washington). Children of American-soldier fathers and Asian mothers are working with Amerasian refugees in the United States to help them find housing and improve their English language skills.

New Orleans Action Corps volunteers focus on recycling projects, using trash and recyclable materials to create public sculptures and murals. They're also planting trees and plants on city river banks.

Border Volunteer Corps (Arizona). A newly funded program to improve living conditions and support environmental and community development along the US-Mexico border. The BVC plans to begin work in Arizona and expand shortly to the other border states.

Public Allies (Chicago, Washington, DC, other cities nationwide). Interns (Allies) between the ages of 18 and 30 receive a stipend ($18,000) plus an education bonus ($5,000). In Chicago, the focus is on housing issues, health care and special needs of at-risk youth. Other cities may differ. Highly competitve program with as many as 35 applicants per position.

Resources

1. *Corporation for National and Community Service.* Ask for the AmeriCorps brochure and list of funded AmeriCorps programs. 1100 Vermont Avenue, NW, Washington DC, 20525, 1-800-94-ACORPS.

2. *National Association of Service and Conservation Corps.* Publishes a directory of eighty youth service and conservation corps, 666 11th Street NW, Suite 500, Washington DC 20001, 202/737-6272.

3. *Voluntary Action — The National Center.* Maintains a network of over 400 affiliated volunteer centers. 1111 North 19th Street, Arlington, VA 22209, 703/276-0542 (Note: There probably won't be any tuition money from work at these volunteer centers, just the satisfaction of helping others in your community!)

Chapter 16
Are Your Parents Eligible?

You may be eligible for financial assistance because your parents were in the military service or presently work for a particular company or belong to a union. A trade group or association can become a source of aid; so can parental membership in patriotic, civic or fraternal associations.

Locating these opportunities will require a systematic approach and considerable parental cooperation. The matrix below can help organize your search strategy

Eligibility Category	Where to Start Looking
Military Service	*Need A Lift?* $3.00 from The American Legion, Attn: Emblem Sales, PO Box 1050, Indianapolis, IN 46206. Also Chapter 13.
Employment	Personnel Director
Union	Secretary of Local or *AFL-CIO Guide to Union Sponsored Scholarships and Awards.* Free for union members. All others should send $3.00 to AFL-CIO Publications Office, 815 16th St., N. W., Rm. 209, Washington, DC 20006.
Trade Group/Trade Associations	Gale's *Encyclopedia of Associations*
Patriotic/Civil/Fraternal Associations	Gale's *Encyclopedia of Associations*

Here are some samples of the kind of information you will uncover. Remember, these are only a few of the many opportunities.

WHERE DO YOUR PARENTS WORK?

Scholarships
Many companies sponsor scholarships for employee children as part of their fringe benefit programs.

Merit scholarships. Approximately 1500 renewable, need-based awards (ranging from $500 to $4,000) sponsored by over 400 corporations for employee children who are Merit Program Finalists (see *The A's & B's of Academic Scholarships*).

General scholarships for employee children. Examples: Westinghouse, RJR Nabisco, The Horace Mann Company (for children of public school employees).

FEEA Fund Scholarships for civilian federal employees and their dependent family members. The 250+ awards range from $300 to $1,200. By June 1. Essay req'd. For an application, send a SASE to the Federal Employee Education and Assistance Fund Scholarship Award, 8441 W. Bowles Ave., Suite 200, Littleton, CO 80123.

Loans

A growing number of large concerns help make it easier for employee children to participate in the Stafford Loan program (see Chapter 10). The companies put up a reserve against loan defaults, then hire firms like United Student Aid Funds to administer the program and find banks to act as lenders. Ford, General Electric, Gillette, Texaco, and Time, are among the 150 that provide this service. To find out if your company has such a plan, ask the employee benefits coordinator or call United Student Aid Funds, 1-800-LOAN-USA.

Federal government employees and dependent family members should request information on FEEA educational loans and scholarships from FEEA, Washington, DC FEEA is a sponsor of five different student loan packages, including TERI loans, a plan in which credit worthy families may borrow up to $20,000 per year. The interest rate floats at 1.5% above prime. FEEA also offers Stafford and PLUS loans. Send SASE to FEEA, 8441 W. Bowles Ave., Suite 200, Littleton, CO 80123.

Savings Plans

RJR Nabisco has exceptional education benefits. The company matches employee contributions (up to $4,000 per child) that are set aside for education. RJR Nabisco also pays the guarantee fee and subsidizes the interest rate for PLUS loan borrowers.

NIKE offers its employees a new savings plan. Participants may deposit up to $1,000 annually per child through payroll deductions. NIKE will match these deposits at a ratio of 25 cents for each $1, with a maximum match of $250 per year, beginning the year the child enters 9th grade. Over the course of four years, NIKE will contribute a maximum of $1,000. NIKE also has an employee scholarship fund that provides need-based awards ranging from $500 to $3,000 to children of full-time employees.

ARE YOUR PARENTS MEMBERS OF

A Trade Group or Association?

Owners and employees of member firms may be eligible. Examples: *National Continental Association of Resolute Employers; National Office Products Association; National Association of Tobacco Distributors.* Look up addresses in Gale's *Encyclopedia of Associations*

A Patriotic/Civic/Fraternal Association?

Among many organizations making awards to members and members' children: *Knights of Columbus; Beta Sigma Phi; 100F/Rebekah; International Order of Job's Daughters; United Daughters of the Confederacy* (61 Awards); Yes — even the *Society for the Preservation of Barber Shop Quartets* has sixteen scholarships. Look up addresses in Gale's *Encyclopedia of Associations*.

A Union?

Examples: AFSCME, American Federation of Teachers, Communications Workers of America, Fire Fighters, Food and Commercial Workers, Teamsters, Letter Carriers, Chemical Workers, Postal Workers, Hotel and Restaurant Employees, Garment Workers, Hospital & Health Care Employees, Seafarers, Machinists, Mine Workers, Transport Workers, etc. Request the *AFL-CIO Guide to Union Sponsored Scholarships, Awards, and Student Financial Aid.* Free to union members. All others should send $3.00 to AFL-CIO Publications and Materials Office, 815 16th Street, NW, Rm. 209, Washington, DC 20006.

Chapter 17
Money from Your Affiliations

Your background, employment record, clubs, associations, religion and nationality may be the key to financial opportunity. Here, as in the previous chapter, you will have to develop a systematic search strategy. The matrix below will help you get started.

THE STUDENT'S MATRIX

Q. Does any job I ever held lead to a financial aid award? (Rule out baby-sitting for grouchy Mrs. Grumpelstein).
A. Check with the personnel office of your present or former employers.

Q. What about my future career? Any hope for a scholarship if I become an engineer?
A. See Chapters 20 and 21 of this publication for some ideas of what you'll find. For a more complete search, consult *Gale's Encyclopedia of Associations* for the addresses of the professional associations that match your career interests.

Q. How about my clubs?
A. Check with chapter/club president or faculty adviser.

Q. What about my religious affiliation? Does my denomination sponsor aid awards?
A. See your minister, priest, or rabbi or write to the national organizations sponsored by the denomination. Addresses in Gale's *Encyclopedia of Associations* in the reference room of the public library.

Q. How about my ancestry or my nationality?
A. Write to the organizations serving your ancestry or your nationality. Addresses in Gale's *Encyclopedia of Associations*.

What will you find? You can strike pay dirt or you can strike out. But even if you have found nothing, there is a reward. You will have learned something about research methods and become reacquainted with the public library which had greatly missed your patronage.

EXAMPLES: JOBS YOU HAVE HELD

Golf Course Caddie

Evans Scholars Foundation. About 200 caddies receive full-tuition and housing scholarships each year. Awards are renewable for 4 years and go to students of outstanding personal character who require financial assistance. Also, candidates must be in the top 25% of their HS class and have caddied for at least 2 years at a WGA member club By Nov. 1. Write Western Golf Association, Evans Scholar Foundation, Golf, IL 60029.

Newspaper Carrier

Thomas Ewing Education Grants for HS seniors who have been *Washington Post* carriers for at least two years; 36 awards ranging from $1000-$2000. By Jan 31. Other newspapers have similar scholarships for their carriers.

EXAMPLES: CLUBS

Boy Scouts
Directory of Scholarships and Loan Funds, a free booklet, lists programs open to scouts and former scouts. Send self-addressed, stamped envelope to: Learning for Life, Boy Scouts of America, 1325 Walnut Hill Lane, Irving, TX 75015.

DECA
Must be member of high school Distributive Education Club of America chapter. Other requirements: financial need; interest in a major in marketing or distribution. Information from chapter advisor.

4-H Clubs & Future Homemakers of America (FHA)
Extensive program for members. 4-H Clubs, for instance, made nearly 300 awards worth $265,000 last year. Contact State Leader (4-H) or State Advisor (FHA).

EXAMPLES: ANCESTRY AND NATIONALITY

NSDAR
Scholarship to children of DAR members who are graduating seniors from an accredited high school. $1,000 annually for 4 years with annual transcript review. Outstanding students may renew for up to an additional 4 years. Applications to National Chairman, DAR Scholarship Committee, Mrs. R. J. Seifert, 4692 Cypress Drive, Brunswick, OH 44212. By Feb. 20.

Descendants of Signers of Declaration of Independence
Must provide definitive proof of direct lineal descent to a signer of the Declaration of Independence to the Society's Registrar-General and become a member of the Descendants of the Signers. Applicant must also be a full-time college student. Requests not naming an ancestor signer will not receive a reply. Annual grants total $10,000 to $11,000, averaging $1,500. Before March 15. Contact Mrs. Phillip Kennedy, Chairperson, DSDA, Inc. Scholarship Committee, 417 East Meadow Lane, Pembroke, NH 03275..

Italian
UNICO National, 72 Burroughs Place, Bloomfield, NJ 07003. Applicant must reside in community with UNICO chapter. By April 15.

Japanese
Japanese American Citizens League, 1765 Sutter Street, San Francisco, CA 94115. Apply by March 1. Undergraduate, graduate. Performing arts, creative arts, law, banking, business.

Polish
Grants Office, The Kosciuszko Foundation, 15 East 65th Street, New York, NY 10021-6595. Polish Studies, music, voice, and others. Mainly specialized, graduate and postgrad study awards. Domestic deadline Jan. 15. Exchange program deadline Nov. 15. Summer Session in Poland (March 15 deadline).

Membership Organizations
Chinese-American Foundation, Danish Brotherhood of America, Lithuanian Alliance, Polish Falcons, Daughters of Penelope, Order of AHEPA, Sons of Norway, Sons of Poland, Russian Brotherhood Organization, Many others. Addresses of all these organizations may be found in Gale's *Encyclopedia of Associations*.

Catholic

The Pro Deo and Pro Patria scholarships. Sixty two awards of $1,500. Father must be member of Knights of Columbus. Must be used at a Catholic college. Application by March 1. Also sponsors other scholarships, fellowships, graduate programs, student loans. Also awards for study in Canada, Mexico, Philippines, Puerto Rico. Contact Director of Scholarship Aid, Knights of Columbus, PO Box 1670, New Haven, CT 06507. Or call, 203-772-2130 x224.

Christian Scientist

Loan program. Range $1,800-$2,500 per academic year. Interest is 3% below prime. Repayment starts six months after graduation. Loans (of up to $1,600 per year) are interest-free to Christian Scientist nurses if they graduate. The Albert Baker Fund, 5 Third St., Suite 717, San Francisco, CA 94103. By July 1.

Jewish

Up to $7,500/year for 2 years. Graduate students preparing for careers in Jewish Community Center work. Write Scholarship Coordinator, JCC Association, 15 East 26th Street, New York, NY 10010. By Feb. 1.

Lutheran

Aid Association for Lutherans

Two competitive programs (1) All College Scholarship Program which offers 800 renewable and nonrenewable awards each year, value range: $500-$2,000. (2) Vocational-Technical School Scholarship program, 50 renewable awards each year to graduating high school seniors. Value range is $500 per year, up to a maximum of 2 years for full-time study and $250 per year, up to a maximum of 4 years for half-time study. Membership in Aid Association for Lutherans is a must. Apply by Nov. 30 to AAL, Scholarships, 4321 North Ballard Road, Appleton, WI 54919.

One noncompetitive program: AAL Lutheran Campus Scholarship. Membership in AAL a must. Awards made by schools. School list may be obtained from above address. From $200-$1,000/year.

Lutheran Brotherhood

Approximately 600 Member Scholarships (value to $2,000). Must be member of Lutheran Brotherhood. By Jan. 29 to Scholarship & Loan Coordinator, Lutheran Brotherhood, 625 4th Avenue South, Minneapolis, MN 55415.

Approximately 500 awards (range $800 to $1,500) to Lutheran students who attend Lutheran junior and senior colleges. Selections made by schools. Awardees do not have to be members of Lutheran Brotherhood. Also a Stafford Student Loan Program Lender.

Methodist

Loans and scholarships for US citizens who have been active, full members of the United Methodist Church for at least one year prior to submitting application. More information from your church or write to: Student Loans & Scholarships, The United Methodist Church, Board of Higher Education and Ministry, PO Box 871, Nashville, TN 37202.

Presbyterian

Scholarships from $100 to $2,000. Undergraduate and graduate. Also grants, loans, and special minority awards. Manager, Financial Aid for Studies, Presbyterian Church in the USA, 100 Witherspoon St., Louisville, KY 40202-1396.

Chapter 18
Money Because You Have Brains and Talent

The SAT has become a national industry. The money spent on designing tests, administering tests, scoring tests, taking tests, teaching tests, coaching tests, disseminating test results, selling the names and scores of test takers to eager college recruiters, interpreting scores, analyzing scores, publicizing scores, and writing about the test, pro and con, places the SAT somewhat below the manufacture of automobiles but far ahead of the value of the horseradish crop as a contributor to our gross national product.

The result of all this energy was unveiled in the spring of 1994. The Scholastic Aptitude Test has a slightly new name — The Scholastic Assessment Test — and a slightly new format. Students will now have to generate answers to some of the math problems on their own (as opposed to guessing via multiple choice). The initial reaction has been a nationwide panic among little Fermat wanabees (and their parents), causing test prep enrollments to double, and our GNP to soar!

On the basis of all evidence, however, this testmania still has no rational underpinnings. It is a modern addendum to the classic treatise "Popular Delusions and the Madness of Crowd." For the SAT is not an intelligence measure. It is not an aptitude measure. Despite its name change, it doesn't really assess anything. It is not a predictor of academic success. And getting high scores on it isn't always important for gaining college admission. It's only verifiable characteristics are that, one, test scores corresponds quite closely to family income. The higher the income, the higher the scores. And two, it thrives on criticism. The more it is attacked and exposed, the more it gains in universality and acceptance.

But this outburst should not turn you away from the test. High scores have a direct monetary application. They can cost you money or they can make money for you.

Cost money? you ask. How? Suppose you live in a school district which emphasizes test coaching and test teaching. That emphasis will raise scores. And higher scores cause property values to soar because parents from everywhere now want to move into your district so that the smarts rub off on junior. Your $50,000 home with a swampy basement, shaky foundation, and a resident population of overweight termite gourmets is suddenly worth $100,000, a nice increase that adds $2,500 to your family contribution. Frankly, we have never understood why enterprising real estate firms don't underwrite SAT preparation courses. It could be their "smartest investment."

Now that we have learned how the SAT can cost you money, let's see how it can make you money. Here is what good scores can do:

1. Qualify you for a National Merit or Regent Scholarship (recent court cases citing racial and gender bias notwithstanding).
2. Push you over the eligibility cutoff for thousands of collegiate academic scholarships.
3. Give you bargaining power when negotiating the content of a financial aid package. Your higher scores make you more valuable to the school because they help raise the average for the entire entering freshman class.

The hard way to raise SAT scores is to find an error in the test and appeal it. An easier way is to wait for the College Board to recenter everyone's scores (the Class of 1996 will be the first to benefit from these new, higher, averages). The easiest way is to take a good SAT preparation course—but take it for the practical reasons listed above and not for any mythological reasons. If a $500 investment in a SAT preparation course can yield a $2,000 no-need scholarship, renewed each year for four years, you have done far better with your money than the shrewdest Wall Street stock picker.

Two national organizations are Stanley Kaplan and The Princeton Review. Their "teaching" styles are very different, but they both have great track records for raising scores. Ask your high school counselor for the nearest test center (or check your phone book). You might also ask about any high school sponsored test prep courses, or local test prep services. The fees will be much lower, and, usually, the results just as good.

WHERE ARE THE REWARDS FOR THE BRIGHT?

The best listing is in *The A's & B's of Academic Scholarships* (see inside back cover). It describes the 100,000 academic awards offered at 1200 colleges; awards that range in value from $200 to $20,000 per year. Most of these awards, moreover, are not based on financial need.

DO YOU HAVE BRAINS, LEADERSHIP, TALENT?

Many scholarship opportunities are reserved for young people with unusual talents and abilities. There are two major ways of linking up with these opportunities: (1) through competitions; and (2) through recommendations of teachers, coaches, bandmasters.

Art and Photography

The Scholastic Art Awards. Cash, scholarships, other. Grades 7-12. The Scholastic Art & Writing Awards, 555 Broadway, New York, NY 10012.

Arts (Dance, Music, Theater, Visual Arts, Writing)

Up to $300,000 in scholarships and cash awards. Also, identification of talented students to colleges who may offer additional awards to prospects. HS seniors or those 17 or 18 years of age by Dec. 1 the year they apply. $35 registration fee. National Foundation for Advancement in the Arts in conjunction with Arts Recognition & Talent Search, 800 Brickell Avenue, #500, Miami, FL 33131. By Oct. 1. (305) 377-1148, (800) 970-ARTS.

Brains

1. *National Merit Scholarship Program.* Participants take the PSAT/NMSQT (usually in their Jr. year of HS). Finalists are contacted by the Merit program through their HS and compete for 2,000 nonrenewable $2,000 scholarships and 4,700 renewable scholarships (worth from $250 to $2,000+ per year for four years). For more information, obtain *PSAT/NMSQT Student Bulletin* from your high school guidance counselor or write the National Merit Scholarship Corporation, 1560 Sherman Ave., Suite 200, Evanston, IL 60201-4897.
2. *National Honor Society.* 250 $1,000 scholarships for members of the National Honor Society. Nominations through HS chapter. February deadline.
3. *Mensa Scholarships.* Awards to $1,000. Based on essay competition. Application from local Mensa group with self-addressed stamped envelope, by January 31.

Citizenship

HS seniors. Entries judged on basis of an application. (1) $1,250 award per Soroptimist region and (1) $2,500 finalist award. Deadline December 15. Contact your local Soroptimist Club or Soroptimist International of the Americas, 1616 Walnut Street, Philadelphia, PA 19103. Make certain to include SASE.

Drama

Thespian Society (majors in theater arts). Members only scholarships. Through HS chapter.

Geography

The National Geography Bee is cosponsored by the National Geographic Society and Amtrak. Top prizes (to fourth- through eighth-grade participants) are three college scholarships worth $25,000, $15,000 and $10,000.

General

Approved list of contests. Ask for Advisory List of National Contests and Activities $4.00, National Association of Secondary School Principals, 1904 Association Dr., Reston, VA 22091.

Leadership & Brains

1. *Century III Leaders Scholarship Program.* $142,000 in scholarships awarded annually. Program is funded by Sylvan Learning Centers and administered by National Association of Secondary School Principals. Program announcement placed in high schools in September. October deadline. Seniors only.
2. *Principal's Leadership Award (PLA).* 150 $1,000 scholarships. Applications sent to high school principal in October. December deadline. Seniors only. Program is administered by National Association of Secondary School Principals.
3. *U. S. Senate Youth Program.* 104 $2,000 scholarships to elected student government officers. Selections by state. Nominations by Nov. 1. William Randolph Hearst Foundation, 90 New Montgomery St., #1212, San Francisco, CA 94105. (415) 543-4057.
4. *Truman Scholars.* $30,000 max. over 4 years. 85 awards. Nominated by colleges in sophomore or junior year. Awards are for junior or senior year plus up to 3 years of graduate school. Solid class standing. Outstanding potential for leadership in the public service. Harry S. Truman Scholarship Foundation, 712 Jackson Place, NW, Washington, DC 20006. Nominations by December 1.

Math, Engineering and Natural Sciences

Barry M. Goldwater Scholarship. Undergraduate scholarships to outstanding college sophomores and juniors who plan to pursue careers in math, engineering or the natural sciences. Tuition, fees, books, room and board, up to $7,000/year for 2 years. One scholarship to a resident of each state. Additional scholars-at-large may also be chosen (233 scholarships were awarded last year). Applicants are selected and nominated by their college. By December 31. Contact your campus faculty representative.

Math, Science and Computer Science

Tandy Technology Scholars. 100 awards of $1,000 each. Final selection based on GPA, SAT/ACT scores, excellence in math, science or computer science, and service to the community. Nominated by HS. For more information, write Tandy Technology Scholars, PO Box 32897, TCU Station, Fort Worth, TX 76129.

Oratory & Essays

Many contests. American Legion, Optimist International, Civitan.

Poetry

The National Library of Poetry awards $12,000 per year to over 250 poets in the North American Open Poetry Contest. Send one original poem (any subject, any style) to the National Library of Poetry, 11419 Cronridge Drive, PO Box 704, Owings Mills, MD 21117. By June 30.

Political Science

First Nationwide Network Scholarship Program. 32 awards of $1,000 each to college juniors majoring in political science, history, or government. Established to honor John F. Kennedy. Essay and application required. Call First Nationwide Network program manager at 507-931-1682 for more information.

Presidential Scholars

No application. No nomination. Approximately 120 students selected from high scorers on the SAT and ACT. Also 20 students picked for achievement in the arts, as identified by the Arts Recognition & Talent Search (see above). A four-day visit to Washington. A handshake from the President. And $1,000 from the Dodge Foundation.

Science

Westinghouse Science Talent Search. HS seniors may enter the competition by submitting a report on an independent research project in science, math or engineering, along with SAT/ACT scores, transcript and application. $205,000 in scholarships, ranging from $40,000 to $1,000. Deadline is early December. For applications contact Science Service, 1719 N Street, NW, Washington, DC 20036. (202) 785-2255.

Sports

In addition to monitoring (and administering) collegiate athletic programs (as described in Chapter 19), the NCAA awards more than $1 million to student-athletes (at Division I, II and III schools) who are pursuing an athletics-related career. Three of the programs are for postgraduates; two are for undergraduates. Request more information from the NCAA, 6201 College Boulevard, Overland Park, KS 66211-2422.

The Unusual?

Can you do bagpipes, Scottish drums or highland flings? Arkansas College has some scholarships for you. Change your kilt for jeans, hop on a Brahma bull, and the National HS Rodeo Association (11178 North Huron, #7, Denver, CO 80234) can present you with a $1,500 rodeo scholarship.

Writing

1. *The Scholastic Writing Awards.* Cash, scholarships, other. Grades 7-12. Schools should have application materials. If not, write The Scholastic Art & Writing Awards, 555 Broadway, New York, NY 10012.
2. *Youth Writing Contest.* High School seniors. (1) $6,000; (1) $5,000; (1) $4,000; and (5) $1,000 scholarships. Electronic typewriters to the top 25 finishers. Write and submit a first person, 1200 word story about a memorable or moving experience you have had, preferably spiritual. Deadline November 28. GuidePosts, 16 E 34th St., New York, NY 10016.

Chapter 19
Money Because You Are an Athlete

A SUMMARY

Athletic scholarships are not limited to those with prowess in the big sports—football, baseball, basketball, hockey, soccer, tennis, and track. There is scholarship money for sailing, badminton, gymnastics, lacrosse, bowling, archery, fencing, rowing, synchronized swimming, skiing and volleyball.

All-star athletes don't need this book. They need an (unofficial) agent who can sort through the offers, enticements, contracts and gifts that come their way. They might need a mechanic, too, to advise them on the relative merits of a Porsche (like Ozzie Guillen) or a Mercedes (like Frank Thomas).

This chapter is for the better-than-average athlete with varsity potential in major and minor sports. What's available for this athlete? How can you link up? Here is the situation in a nutshell:

There is considerable financial aid available at most colleges for students who are good, but not necessarily great, athletes. This aid is either "reserved" for athletes (through designated scholarships) or awarded on a preferential basis as part of the financial aid packaging process.

The key to receiving consideration for this kind of aid lies in the student athlete's determination to market his or her talents. This marketing procedure is based on contacting the appropriate coach at the desired college and getting that coach to shepherd the student's request for admission and financial aid through the bureaucracy of the various institutional admissions and financial aid offices. All college coaches, if convinced of the student athlete's potential contribution to their sport, will take an active role in facilitating the student's admission and financial requests.

For example, some schools have admission representatives whose main responsibility is to coordinate referrals from the athletic department.

Here is a step-by-step outline that students should follow in marketing their athletic talents:

1. Start early. Discuss with your guidance counselor the range of colleges for which you are academically qualified. In selecting suitable schools, keep in mind that approximately 20% of all colleges will reconsider their admission standards to "land" an athlete.
2. Talk to your HS coach about the quality of college athletic programs for which you might qualify. Don't sell yourself short. Coaches need backup players as well as first stringers.
3. Narrow your college selection list to a manageable size, taking into consideration the quality of athletic and academic programs and your "fit" with them. In other words, you *don't* want to be a four-year bench-warmer; you *do* want to be challenged by the school's academic program (but not over- or underwhelmed).
4. Research the name of the coach in your sport at each college on your list. Best source: your high school athletic director's copy of *The National Directory of College Athletics* (there are separate editions of this book for men and women).
5. Draft a personal letter to each coach. This letter should include a profile of your academic interests and achievements. The letter's main part, however, should be a thorough and detailed discussion of your athletic accomplishments and be

supported by statistics, clippings, letters earned, records, and honors. Include mention of any camps or clinics you've attended, and where appropriate, send a videotape of you in action (making certain you're easily identifiable on the tape)! Lastly, indicate you will require financial aid.

6. If your approach elicits interest on the part of the colleges, ask the high school coach to follow up with either a letter of recommendation or a phone call. You may also want to send the college a copy of your scheduled games in case recruiters are in the area!

7. Now you must decide where to apply. Few college coaches will take an interest in you unless your initial letter is followed by a formal application. And remember: here, as with any other application, apply as early as possible.

8. After applying, remain in touch with the college coaches. Inquire about the status of your application and request for financial aid. If possible, visit the college and the coach and sell yourself as a person and as an athlete. Get to know the coach, and make certain his or her coaching philosophy is compatible with your style!

CERTIFICATION

Beginning August 1, 1994, a central clearinghouse began certifying athletic eligibility for Divisions I and II. If you intend to participate in Division I or II athletics as a freshman, you must be certified by this clearinghouse. Essentially, the NCAA wants to make certain all student-athletes are exactly that, and has instituted minimum academic requirements for athletes (e.g., a 2.0 GPA or combined SAT scores of 700). This is the infamous Proposition 48. Your counselors can obtain free registration materials by calling the clearinghouse at (319) 337-1492. Note: Eligibility certification has no bearing on your admission to a particular Division I or II institution.

QUESTIONS & ANSWERS

Q. What do you think of commercial scouting services? How about agents?

A. There are numerous services that represent the student in the search for athletic scholarships. Their fees can be quite high and they generally just follow the eight steps outlined above! (Note: Be careful about these scouts. The NCAA prohibits them from receiving payment based on the amount of your scholarship). There is no reason why you shouldn't "sell" yourself and save the services' fee. As for agents, again be careful. You can jeopardize your college eligibility by agreeing to representation while still in high school or in college.

Q. What is better? Preferential packaging of the aid award or an athletic scholarship?

A. Preferential packaging. If you have a personality conflict with the coach or run into a physical problem that keeps you from competing, you can lose your scholarship. The financial aid package, once it is wrapped up, will hold for a year.

Q. Do you recommend any references for further reading?

A. Yes. The National Collegiate Athletic Association (NCAA) publishes stiff rules on the do's and don'ts of recruiting athletes. It's very important that you know them! Get *The NCAA Guide for the College-Bound Student* from NCAA Publishing, 6201 College Boulevard, Overland Park, Kansas 66211-2422. The brochures are sold in bundles of 50, but you may be able to get a single copy for free. If not, ask the athletic department to order a set...they're fairly inexpensive. Also, get a copy of *The Winning Edge: The Student-Athlete's Guide to College Sports* ($9.00 postpaid) from Octameron Associates. It provides a detailed strategy for taking your sport to college, as well as advice from actual coaches on maximizing your chances for scholarship assistance.

Q. Are college athletic programs really in need of major cleanup?

A. Don't let headlines scare you. Most of the abuses you read about are restricted to the big name football and basketball programs. The fact is, most students who compete in collegiate athletic programs have a higher graduation rate than other students and fare better economically in the job market.

Q. How can I tell which colleges offer scholarships and in what sports?

A. Check the high school guidance office for a copy of *Lovejoy's College Guide*. It lists colleges that offer sports scholarships (broken down by sport). Women should also get *The Women's Collegiate Sports Scholarship Guide* $3.00 from the Women's Sports Foundation, Eisenhower Park, East Meadow, NY, 11554, 1-800-227-3988

Chapter 20
Money for Health Careers

As a budding nurse or doctor or therapist, don't limit your reading to this chapter. Or you will never blossom out into a nurse or doctor or therapist.

You'll find other money sources in different parts of this book. For instance, all the major federal student aid programs (in Chapter 10) will help pay for your medical education. Many of the states (Chapter 11) furnish help in those medical fields in which they believe they have shortages. And there is support for minority medical education. It's described in Chapter 22.

Finally, *Loans and Grants From Uncle Sam* (from Octameron, $6.00, postpaid) goes into all the ins and outs of the major medical loan programs.

FEDERAL SUPPORT FOR THE HEALTH PROFESSIONS

Uncle Sam pours great amounts of money—almost one half a billion dollars per year—into the training of health professionals. The assistance programs fall into two broad categories; those that fund students and those that fund schools which then parcel out some of their money to students.

The individual-based programs are fairly easy to locate. You apply directly to Uncle Sam or through the school you plan to attend. One bit of advice we can give you: You will gain an advantage over fellow applicants if you indicate a willingness to practice your profession in a shortage area. Don't worry about what a shortage area is. Its definition and location will change several times between the time you apply and the time you graduate. What's important to know is that "shortage areas" are a big thing in the operation of the Department of Health & Human Services. It has "primary medical care shortage areas," "dental manpower shortage areas," "rural dental shortage areas," "vision care shortage areas," "podiatry shortage areas," "pharmacy shortage areas," "psychiatric shortage areas," even "veterinary care shortage areas." Can you say "Northern Exposure"?

School-based programs are something else. Here, Uncle demonstrates the technique of buying horses to feed sparrows. The available dollars go directly to schools and usually become part of the faculty payroll (the reason: Medical faculties are high-priced; without federal aid to help pay their salaries, the schools would have to foot the bill alone. To do this, the schools would have to raise tuition so high that no student could afford to enroll). Your challenge is to locate the schools which garnered Uncle's grants and negotiate with deans for some of the lavishings. When writing to the addresses given in the tables that follow, be sure to ask for a current list of funded schools—and be aggressive in your request. The program officers with whom you will deal usually won't understand why you need this information. They think in terms of institutions, not students. You'll have to be polite but tough and persistent.

To save space, we have used the following coding to denote medical fields. Check the coding before entering the table.

A—Allied Health, MA or higher
B—Chiropractic
C—Dentistry
D—Health Administration

E—Medicine
F—Nursing, Associate
G—Nursing, Diploma
H—Nursing, Baccalaureate

I — Nursing, Advanced	R — Podiatry
J — Nursing, Anesthetist	S — Psychology, Clinical
K — Nursing, Community Health	T — Public Health, MA or higher
L — Nursing, Midwifery	U — Safety, Occupational
M — Nursing, Psychiatric	V — Social Work
N — Nutrition	W — Therapy, Occupational
O — Optometry	X — Therapy, Physical
P — Osteopathy	Y — Therapy, Rehabilitation
Q — Pharmacy	Z — Veterinary Medicine

INDIVIDUAL-BASED PROGRAMS

B-C-D-E-O-P-Q-R-S-T-Z. Health Education Assistance Loans. Medical, Dental, Osteopathic, Optometry, Podiatry, and Veterinary Medicine students may borrow $20,000 per year for total of $80,000. Other students: $12,500 per year (limit $50,000). Floating interest rate (91-day Treasury Bill average plus 3%). 6-8% insurance premium. Up to 25 years to repay. Includes Graduate students. Program is not authorized for study at foreign medical schools. Apply through school or write: HEAL, Room 8-29, 5600 Fishers Lane, Rockville, MD 20857.

C-E-O-P-Q-R-Z. Health Professions Student Loan. Tuition plus $2,500 per year. 5% interest. Must show great financial need. Apply through school.

E-I-K-L-P. National Health Service Corps Loan Repayment Program. The program will pay up to $25,000 each year for a minimum 2-year commitment and up to $35,000 per year for years 3 and 4. In addition, for each year served, the program will pay 39% of the participant's outstanding government and commercial education loans towards the increased Federal, State and local income taxes caused by these payments; NHSC Loan Repayment Info, Parklawn Building, Room 7-22, 5600 Fishers Lane, Rockville, MD 20852; 800/ 435-6464, or National Health Service Corps, Loan Repayment Program, US Public Health Recruitment, 8201 Greensboro Drive, #600, McLean, VA 22101, 800/221-9393 (in VA, 703/734-6855).

C-E-I-L-P. National Health Service Corps Scholarship Program. The NHSC will pay tuition, fees, books and supplies, plus a monthly stipend of $796 for up to four years. For each year of support, award recipients owe one year of full-time clinical practice in high-priority health professions shortage areas. For more information, write: NHSC, Scholarship Program, 8201 Greensboro Drive, #600, McLean, VA 22101, 800/221-9393 (in VA, 703/734-6855).

C-E-O-P-Q-R-Z. Exceptional Need Scholarships. All tuition plus stipend. Good for one year only. At completion of year, participants have priority for a NHSC Scholarship. Apply through school.

F-G-H-I-J-K-L-M-W-X-Y. Health Professional Scholarship Program. Scholarships available to second (final) year students in NLN accredited associate degree nursing programs, and upper division baccalaureate or master's degree students in accredited (NLN) nursing, (AOTA) occupational therapy and (APTA) physical therapy programs, on a competitive basis. Benefits include full tuition and fees, monthly stipends and other educational costs. In return for benefits, participants work full-time as professionals in VA medical centers for two years. Applications available March through May from Deans/Directors and Financial Aid Administrators of accredited schools, Chiefs of Nursing or Rehabilitation Medicine at any VA medical center, or Department of Veterans Affairs, Health Professional Scholarship Program (143C2), 810 Vermont Avenue, NW, Washington, DC 20420. (202) 535-7527. By mid-May.

F-G-H-I. Nursing Student Loan Program. Up to $2,500 per year to maximum of $13,000. Need. 5% interest. Apply through school.

All Health Related Fields. Commissioned Officer Student Training & Extern Program (COSTEP) Work Program. For graduate awards, students must have completed minimum of 1 yr. graduate work in medical, dental, veterinary school. For undergraduate awards, students must have completed 2 yrs in a dietary, nursing, pharmacy, therapy, sanitary science, medical records, engineering, physician's assistant, or computer science field. For other health-related areas, students must be enrolled in master's or doctoral program. Student must return to studies following completion of the COSTEP assignment. Serve as an extern (another word for intern) in medical facilities of the Public Health Service during school breaks of 31-120 days duration. Get ensign's pay during work phases. Send for more information. COSTEP, Room 7A-07, Parklawn Bldg., 5600 Fishers Lane, Rockville, MD 20857.(800) 221-9393 or (703) 734-6855.

I-S-W-X-Y. Rehabilitation Training. Monthly trainee stipends. When inquiring, refer to Program 84.129. (Rehab Counseling, Physical and Occupational Therapy, Prosthetics-Orthotics, Speech Language-Pathology, Audiology, Rehab Services to the Blind and Deaf). Employment obligation or payback provisions govern rehabilitation long-term training scholarships. Department of Education, Rehabilitation Services Administration, 400 Maryland Avenue, SW, Washington, DC 20202.

SCHOOL-BASED PROGRAMS

I-J-K-L. Professional Nurse Traineeships. Nurse practitioners, nurse educators, nurse midwives, nurse anesthetist, public health nurses, and other nursing specialties. Tuition, fees, and stipends. Funded through participating schools (most graduate nursing programs participate). Division of Nursing, Room 9-35, 5600 Fishers Lane, Rockville, MD 20857.

D-T. (1) Traineeships in Graduate Programs of Health Administration; (2) Graduate Level Public Health Traineeships. Annual stipends and/or tuition assistance, awarded by the educational institution receiving a grant. Division of Associated and Dental Health Professions, HRSA, 5600 Fishers Lane, Rm. 8C-09, Rockville, MD 20857.

M-S-V. Mental Health Research (biomedical and behavioral). National Research Service awards for individual fellows. Pre-doctoral stipend, $8,500. Post-doctoral stipend is determined by years of experience. Range is $17,000 to $31,500. Grants Management Branch—National Institute of Mental Health, 5600 Fishers Lane, Rm. 7C-15, Rockville, MD 20857.

V. Child Welfare Training Grants. Undergraduate and graduate social work programs or child welfare training programs. Awarded by school. Write for school list. Children's Bureau, 370 L'Enfant Promenade SW, Washington, DC 20447.

U. Occupational Safety & Health Training Grants. Paraprofessional, undergraduate and graduate level. Refer to Program 13.263 (mostly graduate level). Public Health Service, 5600 Fishers Lane, Rockville, MD 20857.

MILITARY MEDICAL AND NURSING PROGRAMS

F. Edward Hebert Armed Forces Health Professions Scholarship Program

Medicine, osteopathy, optometry, clinical psychology (Ph.D.), nurse anesthesia (Master's degree). Monthly stipend plus tuition, fees and books, lab expenses, educational services. Military service obligation. Ask for a scholarship fact sheet from the Assistant Secretary of Defense for Health Affairs, The Pentagon, Washington, DC 20301-1200. For catalogue, write F. Edward Hebert School of Medicine, Admissions Office, 4301 Jones Bridge Rd., Bethesda, MD 20814; 800-772-1743.

Armed Forces Health Professions Scholarship Program

Medicine, osteopathic, dental, optometry, nurse anesthesia (Masters degree). Monthly stipend plus tuition, fees and books, lab expenses, educational services. Minimum three year service obligation. Ask for scholarship fact sheet from Assistant Secretary of Defense (Health Affairs), The Pentagon, Washington, D C. 20301-1200.

Armed Forces Health Professions Financial Assistance Program

Specialized (residency) training for graduate physicians. Annual $15,000 grant plus generous monthly stipend and educational expenses. Service obligation. Each branch of the service has its own point of contact. Write for fact sheets:

Army	Navy	Air Force
HQ, DA (SGPS-PDO) Professionals	Medical Command, US Navy	Directorate of Health
5109 Leesburg Pike, #638	BUMED-512	HQ, USAF Recruiting Service
Falls Church, VA 22041	Washington, DC 20372-5120	Randolph AFB, TX 76150
703-756-8114	202-653-1318	800-531-5980

ROTC Nurse Program (Army, Navy, Air Force)

Students at an approved nursing school affiliated with an Army, Navy, or Air Force ROTC unit. 2, 3, 4 year scholarships; tuition, textbooks, and fees, plus $100/month (Although Army ROTC Scholarships are awarded at an established amount, e.g., 80% of tuition or $7,500/yr., whichever is larger). Service obligation.

Army	Navy	Air Force
Army ROTC	Commander	HQ AFROTC
Attn: ATCC-N	Navy Recruiting Command	Scholarship Actions Section
Ft. Monroe, VA 23651	(Code 314)	551 East Maxwell Blvd.
800-USA-ROTC	801 N. Randolph Street.	Maxwell AFB, AL 36112-6106
	Arlington, VA 22203	
	703-696-4581	

AF ROTC Pre-Health Professions Program

Pre-medicine. Attend a school offering AF ROTC. 2 and 3 year scholarships. Tuition, textbooks, fees, plus $100/month. Service obligation. HQ AFROTC Recruiting Division, 551 East Maxwell Blvd, Maxwell AFB, AL 36112-6106.

PRIVATE PROGRAMS

Dental Assistant

Student Scholarship. $100/$1,000. By Sept. 1. Juliett A. Southard Scholarship Trust Fund, American Dental Assistants Association, 203 North LaSalle Street, #1320, Chicago, IL 60601.

Dental Hygienist

AA, BA, MA, Ph.D. awards to students enrolled in at least second year of dental hygiene program. To $1,500. Also minority program and Proctor and Gamble sponsored program. ADHA Institute for Oral Health, 444 N. Michigan, #3400, Chicago, IL 60611. By May 1.

Dental Lab Technology

Up to 25 scholarships per year. Maximum annual award for dental students is $2,500. Apply by June 15. Maximum annual award for allied dental health students is $1,000. Apply by August 15. ADA Endowment and Assistance Fund, 211 E. Chicago Ave., Suite 820, Chicago, IL 60611.

Laboratory

Several scholarships to help obtain an education in medical lab technology. Limited to International Society for Clinical Laboratory Technology members, or their children. ISCLT Scholarship Committee, 818 Olive St., #918, St. Louis, MO 63101.

Medicine

Research Training Fellowships consist of a $14,000 stipend plus a $4,500 research allowance and a $4,700 institutional allowance. These fellowships enable sixty medical students to do full-time research for one year (renewable for an additional year). Howard Hughes Medical Institute, 4000 Jones Bridge Road, Chevy Chase, MD 20815-6789.

Nursing

Information on scholarships, loans, grants, fellowships, awards. Send $15.95 (postpaid) for the book *Scholarships and Loans for Nursing Education*, Publication No. 41-2638; prepayment must accompany order. National League for Nursing, 350 Hudson St., New York, NY 10014.

Nursing (Advanced)

Scholarship for registered nurses, members of a national, professional nursing association, for advanced degrees. Masters and doctoral. $2,500-$10,000. Full-time student at master's level, full-time or part-time at doctoral level. Send $5 for kit by Feb. 1. Nurses' Educational Funds, Inc., 555 W. 57th St., 13th Floor, New York, NY 10019.

Physician Assistant

For a brochure listing financial assistance sources, write American Academy of Physician Assistants, 950 North Washington Street, Alexandria, VA 22314

Surgical Technology

One $500 award with additional awards available. For students in CAHEA-accredited surgical technology program. Association of Surgical Technologists, 7108-C S. Alton Way, Englewood, CO 80112. By March 1.

Therapy (All)

Graduate and undergraduate scholarships ranging from $1,000 to $1,500 are available to members of Kappa Kappa Gamma. For more information and application materials, contact your chapter's Scholarship Chair, or send a SASE (52 cents) to Kappa Kappa Gamma Foundation, 530 East Town Street, PO Box 2079, Columbus, OH 43216.

Therapy (Occupational and Physical)

Occupational and Physical Therapy scholarships. To students enrolled in accredited school of Occupational or Physical Therapy. Amounts range from $500 to $1,000. Applications from DAR Scholarship Committee, 1776 D Street, NW, Washington, DC 20006-5392. By February 15. The DAR has numerous nursing scholarships as well. Ask for complete listing of awards..

Therapy (Physical, Occupational, Music, Hearing, Audiology, Speech, Pathology and Therapeutic Recreation)

500 awards per year, $500-$1,500 junior/senior undergraduate and graduate scholarships. National AMBUCS Scholarships for Therapists, P.O. Box 5127, High Point, NC 27262. Deadline is April 15.

Therapy (Respiratory)

Various scholarships and awards, $500-$1,250. American Respiratory Care Foundation, 11030 Ables Lane, Dallas, TX 75229. By June 30.

Chapter 21
Money for Other Career Interests

The best way to capitalize on your career interest is through cooperative education (Chapter 12). The next best way is to enroll in a school with a strong reputation in your career field (e.g., Agriculture—*Iowa State*; Hotel Management—*Cornell*). Strong departments usually attract scholarship funds. These funds, however, do not start flowing until you declare your major. The third—and hardest method—is to look for portable scholarships that will fund your major at any accredited school. The list that follows is illustrative, rather than complete. To dig for additional awards, contact (1) the organizations that provide career information in your field of interest (you'll find them in *Need a Lift?*) and (2) the professional associations which serve these careers (locate those in Volume 1, Gale's *Encyclopedia of Associations*). When writing, always enclose a self-addressed, stamped business-size envelope (SASE).

Accounting
1. National Society of Public Accountants. 26 $500-1,000 awards; 1 $2,000 award. Undergraduates only. B or better GPA. Deadline March 10. Nat'l Society of Public Accountants Scholarship Foundation, 1010 N. Fairfax St., Alexandria, VA 22314.
2. Robert Kaufman Memorial Scholarships. Up to 20 awards, ranging from $250 to $5000. Undergrads who plan to pursue an education in accounting can get more information from the Independent Accountants International Education Fund, 9200 S. Dadeland Blvd., Suite 510, Miami, FL 33156. By 28 February.

Architecture
American Institute of Architects offers undergraduate and graduate scholarships. Undergraduate applications through office of the head of an accredited school or its scholarship committee. From $500-$2,500. By Feb. 1. Graduate and professional awards from $1,000-$2,500. No later than Feb. 15th. Applications from AIA, Scholarship Programs, 1735 New York Ave., NW, Washington, DC 20006.

Art & Architecture
Cooper Union (New York City). Extremely competitive admissions. All admitted students receive a full scholarship for the duration of their study.

Education
46 at $1,000 and one $2,000. International grants to HS seniors planning on a teaching career. Scholarship Grants, Phi Delta Kappa, PO Box 789, Bloomington, IN 47402. Request application in October, due by January 31.

Engineering (Civil/Construction)
Various awards. 25-30 undergrad awards of $1,500/yr. for 4 years renewable. Graduate awards of up to $7,500. Director of Programs, AGC Education & Research Foundation, 1957 E St., NW, Washington, DC 20006. By November 15. (202) 393-2040.

Engineering (Materials)
31 $500 scholarships, 3 $1,000 scholarships. Undergrads majoring in materials science and engineering (metallurgy, metallurgical engineering, ceramics, ceramics engineering, polymers, polymer engineering, composites, composite engineering). Citizen of US, Canada, or Mexico. ASM, Materials Park, OH 44073. By June 15.

Engineering (Mining)

100+ scholarships up to $2,000. From the Society for Mining, Metallurgy, and Exploration. Inquire through your college.

Engineering

National Society of Professional Engineers. Top 25% HS standing. US citizen. 3.0 GPA. V-500, M-600. 90 scholarships from $1,000 to $4,000. Financial need; interview. Renewable. Some reserved for minorities, women, and graduate students. NSPE Education Foundation, 1420 King St., Alexandria, VA 22314. By Dec. 1.

Enology & Viticulture

Several awards to graduate students and undergrads (enrolled in a 4-year degree program) majoring in enology or other science basic to the wine and grape industry. Applicants must meet minimum GPA requirements. By March 1. American Society for Enology and Viticulture, PO Box 1855, Davis, CA 95617.

Entomology

Two undergrad scholarships annually. $500 and $1,500. Major in biology, entomology, or related science at recognized school in U. S., Canada, Mexico. Min. of 30 semester hrs. accumulated. Executive Director, Education and Training Committee, ESA, 9301 Annapolis Road, Lanham, MD 20706. By May 31.

Food (Management, Dietetics, Culinary Arts, etc.)

100+ undergrad scholarships. 3.2 GPA. $500-$5,000. Diane Woodworth, Scholarship Services, The Educational Foundation of the National Restaurant Assoc., 250 South Wacker Drive, Suite 1400, Chicago, IL 60606. (312) 715-1010. By March 1.

Food (Management)

Local branches of Assoc.offer $100 to $500 grants totalling $90,000/ year. Internat'l Food Service Executives, 1100 S. State Road 7, #103, Margate, FL 33068. By Feb 1.

Food (Science and Technology)

112 undergrad and grad scholarships. $750-$10,000. Scholarship Dept., Institute of Food Technologists, 221 N. LaSalle St., #300, Chicago, IL 60601. By Feb. 1 for juniors, seniors and graduate students, Feb. 15 for freshmen, and March 1 for sophomores.

Foreign Study

1. *The Rotary Foundation.* Three types of awards: Academic-Year Ambassadorial Scholarships which provide funding (up to $21,500) for one academic year of study in another country (undergrad, graduate or vocational study), Multi-Year Ambassadorial Scholarships which provide a maximum of $10,000 per year for two or three years, and Cultural Ambassadorial Scholarships which are especially for intensive language study (three to six months). Applications must be made through local Rotary Club. To get an application, contact your local club or write: The Rotary Foundation, One Rotary Center, 1560 Sherman Ave., Evanston, IL, 60201. Deadlines determined by individual clubs, and may be as early as March..
2. *The Insider's Guide to Foreign Study* by Benedict Leerburger. Descriptions of 400 programs abroad, including admission requirements, number of credits offered, teaching methods, housing options, and costs. Not much help on financing, but otherwise valuable. Addison-Wesley Publishing Co. (order through bookstores).

Geology

Up to $2,000. Masters and doctoral thesis research at universities in U.S., Canada, Mexico, Central America. Members and nonmembers eligible. Contact Research Grants Administrator, Geological Soc. of America, PO Box 9140, Boulder, CO 80301.

Geophysics

Need and competence. 60-100 awards. Average: $1,200. Students taking course work directed toward career in Geophysics. Scholarship Committee, SEG Foundation, PO Box 702740, Tulsa, OK 74170. By March 1.

Graphic Arts

National Scholarship Trust Fund. Over 100 scholarships ranging from $500-$1,500. Renewable. National Scholarship Trust Fund, 4615 Forbes Ave., Pittsburgh, PA 15213. By Mar. 15. (Some graduate awards as well, ranging from $500 to $4,000. By Jan. 10.)

History

Daughters of the American Revolution. $2,000 per year. Renewable. HS senior. Top third of class. Major in American History. All students are judged on the basis of academic excellence, commitment to the field of study and financial need. All applications must be sponsored by the local DAR Chapter. Send applications to the DAR Scholarship Committee State Chair by 1 Feb. One winner from each state is submitted to the National Chair. For more information, send SASE to: NSDAR, Office of the Committees, attn: Scholarships, 1776 D St., NW, Washington, DC 20006. 202/879-3292.

Home Economics

National and International grants. $1,000-$5,000. Applications from AHEA Foundation, Fellowships, Grants, Awards, 1555 King St., Alexandria, VA 22314.

Horticulture

1. *Bedding Plants Foundation.* $500-$2,000 undergraduate and $1,000-$2,000 graduate scholarships. Renewable. By April 1. Bedding Plants Foundation, PO Box 27241, Lansing, MI 48909. (517) 694-8537. U.S. or Canadian citizen.
2. *American Orchid Society.* Grants for experimental projects and research on orchids. Also biological research, conservation, ecology. $100-$10,000. And fellowship. Up to 3 years working on orchid-related dissertation projects that lead to the Ph.D. degree. Must be enrolled full-time in a doctoral program of an accredited academic institution in the U.S. Fellowship is $9,000/yr. Application by Jan. 1. American Orchid Society, 6000 South Olive Ave., West Palm Beach, FL 33405.
3. *American Horticulture Society.* Year-round internships for students who have obtained or are working toward undergrad degree in Horticulture or related plant science field. Also, information on sources for horticulture scholarships. Send $1.00 and SASE to Education Coordinator, American Horticulture Society, 7931 E. Boulevard Drive, Alexandria, VA 22308.

International Education

1. *Foreign Language and Area Studies* (FLAS) program to stimulate foreign language fluency and develop a pool of international experts. About 600 academic year awards ($8,000 each) and 350 summer fellowships ($1,500 each). Money comes from Uncle Sam. Students apply through funded institutions. For more information and a school list write: Center for International Education, FLAS Fellowships, US Department of Education, Washington, DC 20202-5331.
2. *National Security Education Program.* Federal scholarships for foreign languages and international affairs. Nearly 500 scholarships for undergrads (800-618-6737) and graduate students (800-498-9360).

Journalism

Excellent booklet listing several million in print journalism scholarships. Write for The Journalist's Road to Success: A Career and Scholarship Guide. Has minority section. Dow Jones Newspaper Fund, Inc., PO Box 300, Princeton, NJ 08543-0300. $3.00/copy. 800-DOW-FUND

Librarianship

List of scholarships available for Library Technical Assistants and Librarians. Ask for booklet Financial Assistance for Library and Information Studies, include $1.00. Standing Committee on Library Education, ALA, 50 E. Huron St., Chicago, IL 60611.

Merchant Marine

$750/quarter subsistence allowance for many students at California, Maine, Massachusetts, SUNY, Texas, and Great Lakes Maritime Academies. Service obligation. Academies Program Officer, Maritime Administration, 400 Seventh St., SW, Washington, DC 20590.

Music

Request Scholarship and Awards Chart, listing hundreds of opportunities. Include $1.00 for the chart and postage. Mail to: National Federation of Music Clubs Headquarters, 1336 N. Delaware St., Indianapolis, IN 46202.

Naval Architecture

Ship design. All tuition paid. Top students. High SAT. Webb Institute of Naval Architecture, Crescent Beach Rd., Glen Cove, NY 11542-1398.

Private Club Management

Scholarships. Apply after first year of college. Essay, 2.5 GPA required. The Club Foundation, 1733 King St., Alexandria, VA 22314. By June 1.

Public Service

$500 and $1,000 awards. Careers in Government service. Public Employees Roundtable scholarships. Undergrad and graduate level. Must be working toward degree, 3.5 GPA. Must plan to pursue career in Government. Send SASE to PER, PO Box 14270, Washington, DC 20044-4270, or (202) 927-5000. Applications due by April 15.

Real Estate Appraisers

50 scholarships. $3,000/grad. students, $2,000/undergraduates. Appraisal Institute Education Trust, 875 N. Michigan, Chicago, IL 60611. By March 15.

Science and Engineering

Bell & Howell Scholarships. Electronics, engineering technology, computer science, business. Scores, transcript. 60 $11,000 scholarships ($2,750/yr. for 4 years). Bell & Howell Education Group, Inc., B & H Science & Engineering Scholarship, 1 Tower Lane. Suite 1000, Villa Park, IL 60181.

Special Education

Career preparation at baccalaureate and graduate level — wide range of subjects supporting special education. Program funded through schools. For school list, write: Division of Personnel Preparation, Special Education Programs, Department of Education, Washington, DC 20202.

Teaching

National Teacher Recruitment Program is sponsoring $2,500 scholarships for 1,000 high school seniors who agree to teach in public schools following graduation from college. NTRP, PO Box 47, Washington DC 20044.

Travel

American Society of Travel Agents Scholarship Fund. Undergrad and graduate level, travel schools, junior college, CTC. U. S. or Canadian school. 2.5 GPA, 24 scholarships, $500-3,000. Travel/tourism students. ASTA Scholarship Foundation, Inc., 1101 King St., Alexandria, VA 22314. By June 1.

Vertical Flight

$2,000. Undergraduate and graduate. For career in vertical flight technology. Vertical Flight Foundation, 217 N. Washington St., Alexandria, VA 22314. By Feb. 1.

Chapter 22
Money for Minorities and Women

Many of you have a head start, an edge, in the competition for need-based financial aid. Why? Because, statistically, the income of minority families is less than that of their majority contemporaries, and because the income of women is less than that of men who occupy equal positions. What these numbers say is that for once you have a leg up. You are a stride ahead. Take advantage of that lead.

Only after you have gone the traditional, need-based route, travelled it with savvy and in full control, should you look for the icing, found in this chapter.

In addition, nearly 25% of our nation's colleges and universities have special awards designed to encourage minority enrollment and increase diversity in their student bodies. In fact, there have been veritable bidding wars for the most academically talented minority students (especially those who score above 600 on either part of the SAT) without regard to financial need. Under the previous Administration, the legality of these "race-exclusive" scholarships was questioned when an Assistant Education Secretary announced that they violated Federal civil rights law and that schools awarding such scholarships would no longer be eligible for federal funds. The new Administration feels differently. Race-exclusive scholarships help equalize educational opportunity and improve diversity on the college campus. A diverse educational environment, in turn, benefits all students. After a study by the GAO showed that race-exclusive scholarships made up only 5% of all scholarships awarded to college students, and that they were, in fact, critical to the recruitment and retention of minority students, the Education Department issued its official guidelines: Schools may award race-exclusive scholarships provided their intent is to rectify past discrimination. This more progressive belief (aided by several favorable court rulings) has ended the two-year controversy over race-exclusive awards..

FEDERAL ASSISTANCE TO MINORITIES

All Minorities

Graduate Fellowship Program. Graduate study in science, mathematics, engineering. Master's level and doctorate. Up to three years of support. Approximately $14,400 per year. By early Nov. Write: NSF Graduate Research Fellowship Program, Oak Ridge Associated Universities, PO Box 3010, Oak Ridge, TN 37831.

Legal Training for the Disadvantaged. $3 million program prepares students for entry into law school. $6,000 stipend. Also six week summer institutes and help with law school placement. Write Council on Legal Education Opportunity (CLEO), 1420 N Street., NW, Terrace One, Washington, DC 20005. Apply between Sept. 1 and Feb. 1.

Minority Access to Research Careers. Biomedical science. Funded through schools with substantial minority student bodies. Undergraduate (3rd year) through graduate level. For school list, write to MARC Program, National Institute of General Medical Sciences, National Institutes of Health, 533 Westbard Ave., Westwood Bldg., Room 950, Bethesda, MD 20892.

Minority Participation in Graduate Education Programs. $6 million program to encourage minority students to pursue graduate education. Funded through 73 colleges. For school list write: Office of Higher Education Program Services, Department of Education, 400 Maryland Ave., SW, Washington DC, 20202

Native Americans

Native American Fellowship Program. Need-based program for eligible Indian students in undergraduate programs in business, engineering, natural resources. Graduate programs in education, law, medicine, psychology, natural resources, business, engineering, clinical psychology. All tuition and stipends. Apply through your tribe. Do not apply to the Washington DC office. By Jan. 1.

Indian Health Service Scholarships. Allied health fields to include pharmacy and nursing. Two programs: 1. Preparatory Scholarship Program. Two years. 2. Health Professions Scholarship Program. Both restricted to American Indian, Alaskan native. Tuition plus stipend. Also, a loan repayment program and extern (student) employment program. Apply to Indian Health Service, Twinbrook Plaza, Suite 100, 12300 Twinbrook Parkway, Rockville, MD 20857. By May 1.

Native American Scholarship Fund. Two programs. MESBEC and NALE Programs. (math, engineering, science, business, education, computers). The NALE Program allows Native paraprofessionals in the schools to return to college and complete undergraduate degrees and/or teaching credentials. Students must be admitted or enrolled in college and be seeking a four year degree. Should have high GPAs and high test scores. Contact 8200 Mountain Road NE #203, Albuquerque, NM 87110. (505) 262-2351.

PRIVATE ASSISTANCE FOR MINORITIES

All Minorities

Accounting. Undergraduate and graduate for enrolled students. Approximately 400 merit and need-based awards. Individual grants up to $5,000. Apply by July 1. Manager, Minority Recruitment, American Institute of Certified Public Accountants, 1211 Avenue of the Americas, New York, By 10036-8775.

Architecture. 20 awards, $500-$2,500. Renewable, up to 3 years. Nomination by guidance counselor, school, professional architect. Nomination deadline is Dec 1. Open to HS seniors and college freshmen. Nomination forms from AIA, Scholarship Program, 1735 New York Avenue, NW, Washington, DC 20006.

Dental Hygienists. For at least the second year of dental hygiene curriculum. To $1,500. Also $1,000 for student accepted into entry level dental hygiene program in cert. areas. American Dental Hygienists Assoc., Institute for Oral Health, Suite 3400, 444 N. Michigan, Chicago, IL 60611. By May 1.

Dentistry. 20-30 Scholarships of $1,000 for first year in dental school. By May 1 to American Fund for Dental Health, 211 East Chicago Ave., Suite 820, Chicago, IL 60611.

Engineering. $2 million plus awarded through schools. Schools select. Obtain scholarship guide and list of funded schools from National Action Council of Minorities in Engineering, 3 West 35th Street, New York, 10001-2281.

Engineering. Tuition, fees, stipend of $6,000/academic year, travel to and from summer work site. US citizen. Carry full academic load towards a master's degree in engineering. Must intern at a member employer location during summer. Also, $12,000 stipends for students enrolled in Ph.D. programs. National Consortium for Graduate Degrees for Minorities in Engineering and Science, Inc., Executive Director, GEM Minorities Fellowships, Box 537, Notre Dame, IN 46556. 219-287-1097. By Dec. 1.

Engineering, Computer Science. AT&T Scholarships. Several programs. Most undergraduate awards pay all expenses. Most graduate awards also pay a stipend. For program descriptions, write AT&T Bell Laboratories, ATTN: University Relations, 101 Crawfords Corner Road, Holmdel, NJ 07733-3030. By Jan. 15. Also, summer employment programs.

General Studies. Minority members of the United Methodist Church (for at least 1 year prior) Ethnic Scholarships, value: $100 to $1,000. Contact your church for more information.

General Studies. 1. Student Opportunity Scholarships for Communicant members of the Presbyterian Church, $100-$1,400. By April 1. 2. Native American Education Grant Program for Indians, Aleuts, and Eskimos pursuing post-secondary education. $200-$1,500. By June 1. Other scholarships, grants, loans. Manager, Financial Aid for Studies, Presbyterian Church, 100 Witherspoon St., Louisville, KY 40202-1396.

Geosciences. 35+ scholarships. Undergrad/grad. Undergrad up to $10,000/yr. Graduate to $4,000/yr. AGI-MPP, American Geological Institute, 4220 King St., Alexandria, VA 22302-1507. By Feb. 1.

Geosciences. Some information on private assistance for minorities in the geosciences is also available from Lou Fernandez, Univ. of New Orleans, Lake Front, New Orleans, LA 70122.

Humanities. Tuition plus $10,500 stipend. Up to four years support leading to Ph.D. CIC Pre-doctoral Fellowships Program in Humanities, Kirkwood Hall 111, Indiana University, Bloomington, IN 47405. U. S. Citizen. By Jan.1.

Sciences. CIC Pre-doctoral Fellowships Program in the Sciences, Kirkwood Hall 111, Indiana University, Bloomington, IN 47405. By Jan.1. Will be funded through eligible institution.

Social Sciences. Tuition plus $10,000 stipend. Up to five years support leading to Ph.D. CIC Pre-doctoral Fellowships Program, Kirkwood 111, Indiana University, Bloomington, IN 47405. U.S. Citizen. By Jan.1.

African American

General Studies. National Achievement Scholarship Program for Outstanding Negro Students. African-American students enter the competition by taking the PSAT/NMSQT (in their junior year of HS). Finalists compete for 400 nonrenewable $2,000 scholarships, and about 400 renewable awards (worth $250-$2,000 per year). For more information, see your HS guidance counselor or obtain the PSAT/NMSQT Student Bulletin from the National Merit Scholarship Corp., 1560 Sherman Avenue, Suite 200, Evanston, IL 60201.

Law. Accepted by law school. U.S. Citizen, LSAT, also awards for public interest law. Preferred consideration for need and under 35 years of age. Earl Warren Legal Training Program, 99 Hudson St., Suite 1600, New York, By 10013. By April 1.

Hispanic

Engineering. General Motors/LULAC Scholarship. Thirty $2,000 scholarships to engineering majors with at least a 3.25 GPA. LULAC National Educational Service Centers,, 777 North Capitol St., NE, Suite 305, Washington, DC 20002.

General Studies. LULAC National Scholarship Fund. Students must request scholarship applications from the LULAC council in their community. For list of participating centers, send a SASE to LULAC National Educational Service Centers, 777 North Capitol St., NE, Suite 305, Washington, DC 20002. Currently enrolled students only.

General Studies. Awards to enrolled undergraduate and graduate students with at least fifteen credit hours. SASE to National Hispanic Scholarship Fund, ATTN: Selection Committee, PO Box 728, Novato, CA 94948. Between April 1 and June 15.

General Studies. National Hispanic Recognition Program identifies academically outstanding Hispanic students and furnishes their names to colleges and universities to encourage recruitment and financial support. To be eligible, students must take the PSAT/NMSQT in the fall of their Junior year, identify themselves as being of Hispanic descent, and indicate that they'd like to participate in the program. No monetary awards, but may lead to collegiate awards. Ask your HS counselor for more information, or write: The College Board, National Hispanic Scholar Recognition Program, 1717 Massachusetts Ave., NW, Suite 401, Washington, DC 20036.

Law. 19 $1,000 scholarships and one $2,000 scholarship to students currently attending law school or to student who have been selected to attend the upcoming semester.. Write: MALDEF, 634 S. Spring St., 11th Floor, Los Angeles, CA 90014. By June 30.

Native American

Graduate Study. Over 400 awards per year. Master's, doctorate and professional level assistance to needy students who are at least 1/4 American Indian or enrolled members of federally-recognized tribes. Write: American Indian Graduate Center, 4520 Montgomery Blvd., NE, Suite 1-B, Albuquerque, NM 87109. (505) 881-4584.

PRIVATE AID TO WOMEN

A tip to returning women: If you have small children who require care while you attend class, be sure to let the college know. Your student expense budget should then reflect the child care expense. The larger expense budget increases your need and will help you qualify for more aid.

Aerospace Science or Engineering

Amelia Earhart Fellowship Awards, $6,000 grants for graduate students. Women only. Zonta International Foundation, 557 W. Randolph St., Chicago, IL 60661. By December 1.

Athletics

Complete listing of colleges and universities offering athletic scholarships. Guide is available for $3.00 from Women's Sports Foundation, Eisenhower Park, East Meadow, New York, 11554.

Banking and Business

Scholarships for members only. Write to Financial Women International Scholarships, 7910 Woodmont Ave., Suite 1208, Bethesda, MD 20814-3015.

Career

$5 million annually in local, state, and national awards. Apply early in junior year of high school. America's Junior Miss, Dept. DMO, PO Box 2786, Mobile, AL 36652. Awards count as taxable income.

Engineering

1. Society of Women Engineers. Approximately 40 scholarships, value from $1,000 to $4,000. Society of Women Engineers, 120 Wall Street, 11th floor, New York, NY 10005.
2. Bell Labs Engineering. 15 Scholarships. All college costs. Recommendations from counselor, teachers, principal. AT&T Bell Laboratories, ATTN: ESP Admin., 101 Crawfords Corner Road, Box 1030, Holmdel, NJ 07733. Jan. 15 deadline. Also, summer programs.
3. BPW Loan Fund for Women in Engineering Studies. $5,000 per year, 7% interest. By April 15. For further information and application forms, send SASE with 2 first class stamps to BPW Foundation, 2012 Massachusetts Avenue, NW, Washington, DC 20036.

General

Fellowships and grants for advanced research, graduate study, and community service. Women, US citizen. Application by Nov. 15 for dissertation/postdoc. By Feb. 1 for research and project grants. American Association of University Women, Educational Foundation Fellowships and Grants, PO Box 4030, Iowa City, IA 52243-4030, (319) 337-1716.

Golf

1. Gloria Fecht Memorial Scholarship Fund. $1,500-$2,500 per year academic scholarships for qualified student golfers. Female California residents only. No specific level of golfing skill required. Applications due March 1. Gloria Fecht Memorial Scholarship Fund, 402 W. Arrow Hwy., Suite 10, San Dimas, CA 91773.
2. Women's Western Golf Foundation. Undergraduate scholarships. $8,000 ($2,000/yr.) toward room, board, tuition, fees. Interest in golf is important; golfing ability is not. Selected on basis of academic achievement, financial need, excellence of character. Contact Mrs. Richard Willis, 393 Ramsay Road, Deerfield, IL 60015. By March 1.

Older Women

Four programs, each with its own eligibility requirements. $500 to $2,000. BPW Career Advancement, Avon Foundation Scholarship for Women in Business Studies, New York Life Scholarship for Women in the Health Professions. Wyeth-Ayerst Scholarship for Women in Graduate Medical and Health Business Programs. Apply by April 15. For further information and application forms, send SASE with 2 first class stamps after Oct. 1 to Scholarships, BPW Foundation, 2012 Massachusetts Avenue, NW, Washington, DC 20036, 202/296-9118.

Chapter 23

Special Situations:
The Non-Traditional Student

PHYSICALLY DISABLED

Physically disabled students frequently incur special expenses while attending college. Make sure these expenses are reflected in the student's budget (see Chapter 6). This, in turn, will increase your need and qualify you for more aid.

Your best source of information on special student aid is the Office of Vocational Rehabilitation in your state's education department.

For additional information, write: HEATH Resource Center, One Dupont Circle, NW, Suite 800, Washington, DC 20036-1193. 800-544-3284 or (202) 939-9320. HEATH is the national clearinghouse on post-secondary education for individuals with disabilities, so be specific about your situation to make certain you receive the correct materials. As a start, request their publication entitled *National Resources for Adults with Learning Disabilities.*

Another large clearinghouse is the National Information Center for Children and Youth with Disabilities, PO Box 1492, Washington DC, 20013. Again, the more specific you are with your requests, the more helpful the information you receive will be.

Here are some national programs that provide good work and some assistance:

The Alexander Graham Bell Association for the Deaf, 3417 Volta Place, NW, Washington, DC 20007-2778, sponsors an annual scholarship awards program for profoundly deaf college students. $500 to $1,000. Apply by April 15.

American Council of the Blind offers 16 scholarships ($1,000 to $2,500). By March 15. Contact ACB, 1155 15th St. NW, Suite 720, Washington, DC 20005. 202-467-5081.

National Association of the Deaf. William C. Stokoe Scholarship, annual, $1,000. For deaf students pursuing part-time or full-time graduate studies in a field related to Sign Language, or the Deaf Community. Contact Stokoe Scholarship Secretary, National Association of the Deaf, 814 Thayer Avenue, Silver Spring, MD 20910. Deadline March 15.

Recording for the Blind. Learning Through Listening Awards to HS seniors with specific learning disabilities who plan to continue their education. Three awards, $3,000 each. By February 1. Contact: Public Affairs Department, Recording for the Blind, 20 Roszel Road, Princeton, NJ 08540.

Sertoma International. Scholarship Program for hard of hearing students pursuing four-year college degrees. Five awards, $1,000 each. Applicants must have documented hearing loss and be a full-time entering or continuing student. By May 1. SASE to Otican/Phonic Ear Scholarships, c/o Sertoma (SERvice to MANkind), 1912 East Meyer Blvd., Kansas City, MO 64132-1174.

PART-TIMERS

Most financial aid is based on being at least a half-time student. But take heart. Uncle's definition of "half-time" is more generous than that of most schools, therefore, we urge you to apply for federal student aid even if you aren't sure what your status will be (see Chapter 10). Also, under current law, colleges can set aside 10% of their SEOG and CW-S fund for assistance to less than half-time (i.e., part-time) students. Several states also help part-timers, so check with them as well (addresses in Chapter 11).

Our Suggestion: If at all possible, take an additional course, and boost your status to half-time.

118

ARE YOU 50, 60 OR OLDER?

If you plan to be at least a half-time student, you should remember that financial aid is awarded on the basis of need and not age. Hence, you can freely compete with those who are just out of high school and anybody else for all available financial aid.

If you plan to take just a few courses, you should know that many schools offer reduced tuition for older citizens. Many will even let you attend courses for free or on a space available basis. At least three states (Alabama, South Carolina and New Mexico) also offer reduced tuition for older citizens. Check your local college or your state higher education office.

Two other sources of college information for older students are The Institute of Lifetime Learning, American Association for Retired Persons, 1909 K Street NW, Washington DC, 20049 and Adult Learning Services, The College Board, 45 Columbus Avenue, New York, NY 10023. **Note:** These are not scholarships sources, just helpful resources!

ARE YOU ONLY 25?

Over 39% of all college students are 25 or older (16% are 35 or older). Now, these 7 million students have their own association, The National Association of Returning Students. Write for information on their newsletter and list of resources. PO Box 3283, Salem OR 97302; or call 503-581-3731.

Chapter 24
A Few Words About Grad School

Graduate student aid falls into three main categories: Fellowships, assistantships and loans. Neither fellowships nor assistantships need to be repaid, however both usually require some sort of service (for example, conducting research, working with faculty or teaching undergraduates). Most students rely on a combination of these three aid sources, however, Doctoral candidates are most likely to receive fellowships and assistantships, Master's students are most likely to receive a balance of assistantships and loans, and professional students are most likely to receive loans. Further analysis of graduate student aid shows that of Master's students, those in law, medicine and business have the largest loans. Those in engineering and the natural sciences receive the largest assistantships, and those in the natural sciences, medicine and the social sciences receive the largest fellowships. Similarly, of Doctoral students, those in medicine have the largest loans, those in engineering and the natural sciences receive the largest assistantships, and those in the natural sciences, medicine and the humanities receive the largest fellowships.

70% OF ALL GRADUATE AID
To learn where 70% of all graduate aid is, you will have to go back to the beginning of this book.

First, you must enhance your eligibility for aid. The lessons in Chapters 4 through 7 are as applicable to the graduate student as they are to the college-bound.

Second, review Chapter 10 and become familiar with the major sources of aid available to you: the Stafford Loan, the Perkins Loan and College Work-Study. If your future is in a medical field, add Chapter 20 to your reading.

NOTE: Graduate students are not eligible for Pell Grants or SEOGs.

3% OF ALL GRADUATE AID
For 3% of all graduate aid, check with your home state. Alabama, Alaska, Arizona, California, Colorado, Connecticut, Delaware, DC, Florida, Idaho, Illinois, Iowa, Maryland, Michigan, Mississippi, Nevada, New Hampshire, New Jersey, New Mexico, New York, North Carolina, Ohio, Oklahoma, Texas, Vermont, Virginia, Washington, Wisconsin and Puerto Rico will offer a combined total of about $40.7 million to help 27,722 graduate students. $29.3 million is in need-based aid (to 23,100 students); $11.4 million is in non need-based aid (to 4,600 students).

This money is not evenly distributed among the states. For example, New York alone awards $15.6 million to graduate students!

Also, be aware that many of these opportunities are sharply restricted in terms of major field of study (e.g., medicine, law, dentistry) or population group which benefits (e.g., minority). Furthermore students must usually enroll in a school located in the state.

10% OF ALL GRADUATE AID
About 10% of all graduate aid is dispersed throughout this book. For instance, if you get a commission in the military and are willing to extend your period of service, you may qualify for graduate training.

The cooperative education route (Chapter 12) is rich in graduate opportunities. And you'll find more in Chapters 21 and 22.

12% OF ALL GRADUATE AID

For 12% of all graduate support you must talk to the department chairperson or dean at the school where you plan to pursue your graduate studies. Here is how these people can help you:

- With departmental scholarships and grants
- With graduate assistantships
- With internships and summer jobs
- With employment funded by a grant

Remember, in most instances, the professor gets the grant, but will need grad students to help count the chromosomes and wash out the test tubes.

1% OF ALL GRADUATE AID

That you have to discover yourself. Through research. The best bet starting points for research: two publications put out by the Foundation Center and one by the Oryx Press:

1. The Foundation Center's current *Foundation Directory*.
2. The Foundation Center's current *Foundation Grants to Individuals*.
3. The Oryx Press' current *Directory of Grants in the Humanities*.

We don't recommend you buy either reference. They are expensive. But do locate them in the reference room of the library and spend some time looking through them.

4% OF ALL GRADUATE AID

All Disciplines

Request *A Selected List of Fellowship Opportunities and Aids to Advanced Education* from The Publications Office, National Science Foundation, 4201 Wilson Blvd., Arlington, VA 22230. This booklet contains information on fellowship opportunities for US citizens and foreign nationals in many fields of study (including the humanities, social sciences, engineering, physical sciences, math, and life/medical sciences). Undergraduate, graduate, post-doctoral.

Engineering and Science

Support of graduate education by the Department of Defense. Stipends and tuition. No service obligation. 1. Navy: ASEE, 11 DuPont Circle, Suite 200, Washington, DC 20036. (202) 986-8525. 2. Air Force: SCEEE, Fellowship Program, 1101 Massachusetts Ave., St. Cloud, FL 34769. 3. NDSEG Fellowship Program, 200 Park Drive, Suite 211, PO Box 13444, Research Triangle Park, NC 27709, Attn: Dr. George Outterson.

Engineering and Science

Fellowships. College seniors for graduate study. US citizenship required. Grad study at selected universities. GPA must be 3.0/4.0. Most on a work-study basis. Spend summer vacation working at Hughes Aircraft Co. Tuition, fees, stipend, travel and relocation expenses, salary for summer and other periods of full-time work. Hughes Aircraft Company, PO Box 80028, Bldg. C1/B168, Los Angeles, CA 90080-0028. (310) 568-6711.

Food and Agricultural Science

National Needs Graduate Fellows. Master's and doctor's level. Funded through school. For school list, write: US Office of Education, 400 Maryland Avenue, SW, Washington, DC 20202.

Graduate Fields

Graduate and Professional Study. Fellows pay no tuition or fees. $21 million program. (1) Patricia Roberts Harris Graduate Study Fellowships. Awards designed to increase participation of minorities and women who are underrepresented in academic/professional fields. (2) Patricia Roberts Harris Public Service Education Fellowships. Master's and doctorate level. Fellows selected by schools. Up to $14,000 stipend for 12 months for both programs. For school list, write: Graduate Programs Branch, Department of Education, 400 Maryland Avenue, SW, Washington, DC 20202-5251.

Humanities

Eighty awards (one-year only) for students entering a program leading to a Ph.D. in preparation for careers of teaching and scholarship in the humanities. Tuition plus $13,250 stipend. Applications must be requested by November 12. To get an application, you must provide the following information: Full name, mailing address, city and state, telephone number, location in February-March 1995, undergraduate institution, undergraduate major, year of graduation, and intended discipline in graduate school. Send all this to: Mellon Fellowships, Woodrow Wilson National Fellowship Foundation, CN 5329, Princeton, NJ 08543-5329.

Humanities, Arts, Social Sciences

Javits Fellowships. $8 million program. About 56 fellowships of up to $14,000 per year. Contact: Graduate Programs Branch, Department of Education, 400 Maryland Avenue, SW, Washington, DC 20202.

International Business

Some student fellowships. 35 awards. Funded through schools. For school list, write: Office of International Studies Branch, Department of Education, Rm. 3054, ROB-3, 400 Maryland Avenue, SW, Washington, DC 20202.

International Exchange

Possession of B.A. degree. Live and study abroad as a Fulbright student. Write IIE, US Student Programs, 809 UN Plaza, New York, NY 10017. (212) 984-5330.

Languages and Teaching

Graduate fellowships for foreign language and area studies. Over 130 programs participate. Funded through schools. Schools select students. Tuition and stipends. Direct inquiries to university of choice; if necessary, for school list, write: Center for Internat'l Education (FLAS), US Dept.. of Education, Washington, DC 20202-5331.

Librarianship

Library and Human Resource Development Program. Funded through schools. Schools select students. For school list, write: Discretionary Library Programs Division, OERI, Dept. of Education, 555 New Jersey Avenue, NW, Washington, DC 20208-5571.

Marine Sciences

Marine Sciences. The National Sea Grant College Federal Fellows Program. Program funded by National Sea Grant College Program Office. For students who are in a graduate or professional degree program at an accredited institution of higher education. Request brochure from National Sea Grant College Program Office, Attn: Fellowship Director, 1335 East West Highway, Silver Spring, MD 20910.

Medical and Biological Sciences

Scholarships and Fellowships. Howard Hughes Medical Institute. College seniors or first-year graduate students. Study leading to doctoral degrees in biological/medical sciences. 66 awards per year, consisting of $14,000 stipend plus $12,700 cost-of-education allowance to the fellowship institution. Renewable for up to five years. Office of Grants and Special Programs, Howard Hughes Medical Institute, 4000 Jones Bridge Road, Chevy Chase MD 20815. (301) 215-8889.

Music
The American Musicological Society offers 5 dissertation fellowships per year. Twelve-month stipend (nonrenewable) of $10,000. Application forms from Secretary, AMS Fellowship Committee, Department of Music, New York University, 268 Waverly Building, Washington Square, New York, NY 10003. By October 1.

National Needs Areas
Stipends of $14,000 to enhance teaching and research in designated academic needs areas (current examples — math, science, and foreign languages). These awards go to graduate students of superior ability who demonstrate financial need. $25 million program funded through 84 different schools. For listing, write Division of Higher Educational Incentive Programs, Office of Post-secondary Education, Department of Education, Rm. 3022, 400 Maryland Avenue SW, Washington, DC 20202-5339.

Psychology
Two awards of $2,500 each for full-time doctoral students in psychology who are ethnic minorities and accepted into an accredited California school. By Oct. 15. California Psychological Association Foundation, 1010 11th Street, Suite 202, Sacramento, CA 95814. *Students outside California should contact their own state's affiliate of the American Psychological Association to inquire about scholarship assistance.*

Science, Social Science, Math, Engineering
Graduate study in sciences, social sciences, mathematics and engineering. Three separate competitions: Graduate Research Fellows, Minority Graduate Fellowships and Women in Engineering Fellowships. Three years of support. Approximately $14,000 per year. 750 new fellows yearly. For more information (and a catalogue), write Oak Ridge Associated Universities, PO Box 3010, Oak Ridge, TN 37831-3010). First deadline is early November.

Space-Related Science and Engineering, Aerospace Research
Awards up to $22,000. Renewable. Graduate students. Also summer programs. For more information: Graduate Student Researchers Program, Higher Education Branch, Education Division, NASA Headquarters, Washington, DC 20546. Also, graduate and doctoral fellowships at affiliated schools. For more information: Space Grant College and Fellowship Program, University Programs Branch, Mail Code FEH, NASA, Washington, DC, 20546. 202/453-8344.

IF ALL THIS DOESN'T COVER YOU
Investigate the commercial loan sources listed in Chapter 7. The combination of these loans and Stafford loans (Chapter 10) should be more than enough to cover education costs. In most instances, you have the option to defer payment while in school, and then take up to twenty-five years to repay after deferment.

Chapter 25
A Treasure Chest of Tips

In an ideal world, students could hope that if things were tight one year, the next year would be better, with more federal money flowing their way. Unfortunately, that's not likely. Students today must cope with level aid funding while tuitions keep rising.

For these students, the slogan is "know more about every aspect of financial aid or dig deeper." To save you the purchase of a new shovel, here is a summary of the financial aid skills you, as a student today, must master.

1. Selecting a College (I). When picking a college, go beyond the normal search criteria, such as majors offered, academic reputation, and distance from home, and inquire about innovative tuition aid features. These may include matching scholarships, sibling scholarships, guaranteed cost plans, installment plans, special middle income assistance programs, tuition remission for high grades, etc. See Chapter 9.

2. Selecting a College (II). All factors being equal, pick colleges most likely to offer you a financial aid package rich in grants and scholarships you don't have to repay. Such a package is a lot better than one made up of loans which will saddle you with a repayment burden for many years after graduation. Best bet: Any school in which your academic record places you in the upper 25% of the profile of the incoming freshman class. See Chapters 7 and 9.

3. Selecting a College (III). Always send applications to two colleges of equal merit. If you get accepted by both, you might be able to play one against the other in securing a more favorable package. See Chapters 7 and 9.

4. Try the External Degree Route. Here you win a sheepskin from an accredited school without ever leaving home or job. Such a diploma will cost less in money and time than if it had been earned through campus attendance. External degrees offer academic credit for documented learning and experience you have already acquired, and couples these with formal assessments. See Chapter 7.

5. Do Four Years Work in Three. You must attend summer school, but the compressed time will save you the "inflationary increase" of the fourth year. On a similar note, try not to spend extra years getting through college. Fewer and fewer students are graduating in four years...costing them a whole extra year's tuition.

6. Spend Some Time at a Community College. Work hard. Get good grades. Transfer to a solid four-year institution. This way, you can pick up the halo of a prestige diploma at half the cost.

7. Understand How Need Analysis Works. By knowing the formulas, the shrewd family can present its financial picture in such a way as to obtain a more favorable need analysis. This isn't unlike the method used for presenting one's financial picture to the IRS so as to qualify for the smallest possible tax liability. See Chapters 6 and 7.

8. Try Some "What If?" Calculations. But first, learn how need analysis works. A typical "what if": Is this a good time for mom or dad to finish their college work, along with son and daughter? Or will it be more advantageous, financially, for your parent to go back to work and help with expenses? You'll be surprised at the dollar figures generated by "what if" drills. See Chapter 7.

9. Don't Pass Up the Entitlement Programs. Billions in low-interest, subsidized federal student loans go unused each year simply because students think they are ineligible, don't bother to go through the paper work hassle, or just don't know about the program. See Chapter 10 and *Loans and Grants From Uncle Sam* (inside back cover).

10. Cash Flow (I). Search for a low-interest, private loan. Numerous states have set up loan authorities which float tax-exempt bonds to raise student loan money. And colleges themselves have received permission to issue such bonds. At the same time, private banks are becoming more innovative in sponsoring combination savings/lending plans. Keep an eye out for these developments. They can help middle-income families with the cash flow problem of paying for college. See Chapters 6, 7, and 9.

11. Cash Flow (II). Go to college on the house. Many home owners have accumulated large amounts of equity in their houses and they want to put it to work. Your strategy: Releasing this equity either through a line of credit or through refinancing the first mortgage. See Chapters 7 and 9.

12. Negotiate With the Financial Aid Administrator. The FAA will present you with a package of assistance that should, in theory, cover the difference between what college costs and what your family can contribute. If you feel the college really wants you, because you are a brain or an athlete or the child of an alumnus or can help with meeting a geographic or minority quota, you may want to negotiate the content of the package. Your objective: To increase the grant component (money that doesn't have to be repaid) and reduce the loan component (money you must repay). See Chapters 6, 7, and 9 and *Financial Aid Officers* (inside back cover).

13. Try for an Academic Scholarship. Over 1200 colleges offer academic scholarships to students with a B average and SAT scores of 900 or more. Middle income folks take notice: Most of these scholarships are not based on financial need. If you are just outside the SAT eligibility range for one of these awards, take a good SAT preparation course. It may raise your scores enough to enter the winner's circle. See Chapter 18 and *The A's and B's of Academic Scholarships* (inside back cover).

14. Go the Cooperative Education Route. Over 900 colleges offer co-op education programs. Alternate formal study with periods of career-related work. Earn up to $7,000 per year during the work phase. It may take an extra year to win the degree, but it will be easier on the pocketbook. See Chapter 12 and *Earn & Learn* (inside back cover).

15. Athletic Student Aid. We aren't talking about the "Body by Nautilus, Mind by Mattel" tackle who can do 40 yards in 4 seconds. Husky U. will find that person. We're talking about students who are better than average in a variety of sports, ranging from tennis to golf to lacrosse. A great many colleges seek people who can be developed into varsity material. The rewards come in two forms: outright scholarships or an "improved" financial aid package. See Chapter 19.

16. Acceleration. Can you get credit for a semester or a year of college work? You can through the Advanced Placement Program or by enrolling in college courses in high school. When credits can cost as much as $300 each, receiving tuition credit for academic credit leaves money in the bank.

17. Be An Accurate, Early Bird. Be as accurate as possible in filling out financial aid forms. Submit them as early as you can. When resources are tight, it's first-come, first-served. Those who must resubmit their forms and those who are slow in applying come in at the end of the line. By then, all the money is gone. See Chapters 6 and 7.

18. Check the Military Offerings. Reserve enlistments are especially attractive. For a hitch in the National Guard you can pick up a state benefit, a federal bonus, partial loan forgiveness, drill pay, sergeant stripes (if you also participate in ROTC), and in some cases, tuition remission at the state university. And these are not either/or opportunities. You can have most of them, or all of them. See Chapter 13.

19. Take Advantage of Teacher Mania. Individual colleges, most states, and Uncle Sam all have loan forgiveness programs for prospective teachers. Go this route and your education will cost you very little. You teach Ohm's law for four years to pay off the obligation. You pick up a little maturity, a lot of patience. You contribute to the well-being of hundreds of scholars-to-be. And you're still young enough to begin a different career if teaching is not for you. Chapters 9 and 11.

20. Sacrifice. You may have to give up a few luxuries: Cancelling your pet's Beverly Hills grooming sessions can save you $3,200 per dog per year; using a Volkswagen instead of your Lear jet can save you $540 per tank of gas.

Appendices

Appendix 1

FAMILY CONTRIBUTION FOR DEPENDENT STUDENTS (1995/96 ACADEMIC YEAR)

PARENTS' CONTRIBUTION FROM INCOME

1. Parents' Adjusted Gross Income .... $ _____
2. Parents' Untaxed Social Security Benefits .... $ _____
3. Parents' Aid to Families With Dependent Children Benefits .... $ _____
4. Parents' Other Nontaxable Income. This may include child support received, worker's compensation, disability payments, welfare benefits, tax-exempt interest income, housing, food and living allowances for military, clergy or others .... $ _____
5. IRA, KEOGH, and 401(k) payments made by parents. .... $ _____
6. **Total Income.** Add Lines 1 through 5. .... $ _____
7. US and State Income Taxes paid .... $ _____
8. Social Security Taxes paid .... $ _____
9. Child Support paid by you for another child .... $ _____
10. Income Protection Allowance from Table A .... $ _____
11. Employment Expense Allowance. If both parents work, enter 35% of the lower income or $2,500, whichever is less. If your family has a single head of household who works, enter 35% of that income or $2,500, whichever is less. .... $ _____
12. **Total Allowances.** Add Lines 7 through 11 .... $ _____
13. **Parents' Available Income.** Line 6 minus Line 12 .... $ _____

PARENTS' CONTRIBUTION FROM ASSETS*

14. Cash and Bank Accounts .... $ _____
15. Other Real estate, investments, stocks, bonds, trust funds, commodities, precious metals (less any investment debt) .... $ _____
16. Business and/or Commercial Farm Net Worth from Table B .... $ _____
17. **Total Assets.** Add Lines 14 through 16 .... $ _____
18. Asset Protection Allowance. From Table C .... $ _____
19. Discretionary Net Worth. Line 17 minus Line 18 .... $ _____
20. **CONTRIBUTION FROM ASSETS.** Multiply Line 19 by 12%. If negative, enter $0 .... $ _____

PARENTAL CONTRIBUTION

21. Adjusted Available Income. Add Lines 13 and 20............................$_____
22. **PARENT CONTRIBUTION.** From Table D. If negative, enter 0. ....$_____
23. Number in College Adjustment. Divide Line 22 by the number in college (at least half-time) at the same time. Quotient is the contribution for each student...$_____

STUDENT'S CONTRIBUTION FROM INCOME

24. Student's Adjusted Gross Income..$_____
25. Untaxed Social Security Benefits ....$_____
26. Other Untaxed income and benefits. See Line 4. Also include cash support paid on your behalf from non-custodial parent, or any other person...$_____
27. Total Income. Add lines 24, 25, and 26..$_____
28. US Income Taxes paid..$_____
29. State Income Taxes paid. ....$_____
30. Social Security Taxes paid. ....$_____
31. Income Protection Allowance. Enter $1,750. ....$_____
32. Total Allowances. Add Lines 28 through 31.....................................$_____
33. Students Available Income. Line 27 minus Line 32..........................$_____
34. **STUDENT'S CONTRIBUTION FROM INCOME.** Multiply Line 33 by 50%. ....$_____

STUDENT'S CONTRIBUTION FROM ASSETS*

35. Add all of student's assets—cash, savings, trusts, investments, real estate (less any investment debt)...$_____
36. **STUDENT'S CONTRIBUTION FROM ASSETS.** Take 35% of Line 35. ....$_____

FAMILY CONTRIBUTION

37. If one student is in college, add lines 22, 34, and 36.........................$_____
38. If two or more students are in college at the same time, add for each, Lines 23, 34, and 36..$_____

*Contribution from student and parent assets will equal $0 if Parents' AGI (Line 1) is less than $50,000 and the family was eligible to file a 1040A, 1040 EZ, or no tax return at all.

Appendix 2

FAMILY CONTRIBUTION FOR INDEPENDENT STUDENTS WITH DEPENDENTS (1995/96 ACADEMIC YEAR)

CONTRIBUTION FROM INCOME

1. Student's (and Spouse's) Adjusted Gross Income........................... $_____
2. Student's (and Spouse's) Untaxed Social Security Benefits........... $_____
3. Student's (and Spouse's) Aid to Families With Dependent Children Benefits... $_____
4. Student's (and Spouse's) Other Nontaxable Income. This may include child support received, worker's compensation, disability payments, interest on tax-exempt bonds, welfare benefits, cash support from others, housing, food and living allowances for military, clergy or others........................ $_____
5. IRA, KEOGH, 401 (k) Payments made by Student (and Spouse).... $_____
6. **Total Income.** Add Lines 1 through 5................................... $_____
7. US and State Income Taxes paid. .... $_____
8. Social Security Taxes paid .... $_____
9. Child support paid by you for another child............................. $_____
10. Income Protection Allowance from Table A.............................. $_____
11. Employment Expense Allowance. If both student and spouse work, enter 35% of the lower income or $2,500, whichever is less; If student qualifies as head of household, enter 35% of income or $2,500, whichever is less... $_____
12. **Total Allowances.** Add Lines 7 through 11............................... $_____
13. **Available Income.** Line 6 minus Line 12. .... $_____

CONTRIBUTION FROM ASSETS (Student's and Spouse's)

14. Cash and Bank Accounts.. $_____
15. Other Real estate, investments, stocks, bonds, trust funds, commodities, precious metals (less investment debt)...................... $_____
16. Business and/or Commercial Farm Net Worth from Table B. .... $_____
17. **Total Assets.** Add Lines 14 through 16................................... $_____
18. Asset Protection Allowance. From Table E. .... $_____
19. Discretionary Net Worth. Line 17 minus Line 18......................... $_____
20. **CONTRIBUTION FROM ASSETS*** Multiply Line 19 by 12%. If the result is a negative value, enter $0........................... $_____
21. Adjusted Available Income. Add Line 13 and Line 20.................. $_____
22. **TOTAL CONTRIBUTION.** From Table D. .... $_____
23. Number in College Adjustment. Divide Line 22 by the number in college (at least half-time) at the same time. Quotient is the contribution for each student.. $_____

*Contribution from assets will equal $0 if Student and Spouse AGI (Line 1) is less than $50,000 and the student (and spouse) were eligible to file a 1040A or 1040EZ.

Appendix 3

FAMILY CONTRIBUTION FOR INDEPENDENT STUDENTS WITHOUT DEPENDENTS OTHER THAN A SPOUSE (1995/96 ACADEMIC YEAR)

CONTRIBUTION FROM INCOME

1. Student's (and Spouse's) Adjusted Gross Income............................$_____
2. Student's (and Spouse's) Untaxed Social Security Benefits...........$_____
3. Student's (and Spouse's) Welfare Benefits. ....$_____
4. Student's (and Spouse's) Other Nontaxable Income. This may
   include child support received, worker's compensation,
   disability payments, interest on tax-exempt bonds,
   welfare benefits, cash support from others, housing, food
   and living allowances for military, clergy or others.......................$_____
5. IRA, KEOGH, 401 (k) Payments made by Student (and Spouse).....$_____
6. **Total Income.** Add Lines 1 through 5...$_____
7. US Income Taxes paid..$_____
8. State Income Taxes paid ....$_____
9. Social Security Taxes paid. ....$_____
10. Income Protection Allowance of $3,000 for single students or
    married students if both student and spouse are enrolled in
    college at least half time; $6,000 for married students if only
    one is enrolled at least half-time. ....$_____
11. Employment Expense Allowance. If the student is
    single, enter $0. If the student is married and both the student
    and spouse are working, enter 35% of the lower income
    or $2,500, whichever is less. Otherwise enter $0...........................$_____
12. **Total Allowances.** Add Lines 7 through 11...................................$_____
13. **Available Income.** Line 6 minus Line 12. ....$_____
14. **Contribution from Income.** Take 50% of Line 13. ....$_____

CONTRIBUTION FROM ASSETS (Student's and Spouse's)

15. Cash and Bank Accounts. ....$_____
16. Other Real estate, investments, stocks, bonds, trust funds,
    commodities, precious metals (less any investment debt)...............$_____
17. Business and/or Commercial Farm Net Worth from Table B. ....$_____
18. **Total Assets.** Add Lines 15 through 17...$_____
19. Asset Protection Allowance. From Table E. ....$_____
20. Discretionary Net Worth. Line 18 minus Line 19............................$_____
21. **CONTRIBUTION FROM ASSETS*** Multiply Line 20 by
    35%. If negative, adjust to 0. ....$_____
22. **TOTAL CONTRIBUTION.** Add Line 14 and Line 21......................$_____

* Contribution from assets will equal $0 if Student (and Spouse) AGI (Line 1) is less than $50,000
and the student (and spouse) were eligible to file a 1040A or 1040EZ.

REFERENCE TABLES

TABLE A—INCOME PROTECTION ALLOWANCE

Family Members (Including Student)	Allowance
2	$11,150
3	13,890
4	17,150
5	20,240
6	23,670
Each Additional	2,670

Note: *For each student over one in college, subtract $1,900 from the appropriate maintenance allowance.*

TABLE B—ADJUSTMENT OF BUSINESS/ FARM NET WORTH

Net Worth of Business/Farm	Adjustment
To $80,000	40% of Net Worth
$80,001 to $240,000	$32,000, plus 50% of NW over $80,000
$240,001 to $400,000	$112,000, plus 60% of NW over $240,000
$400,001 or more	$208,000 plus 100% of NW over $400,000

TABLE C—ASSET PROTECTION ALLOWANCE, DEPENDENT STUDENT

Age of Older Parent	Two-Parent Family	One Parent Family
40-44	$36,100	$25,300
45-49	40,900	28,300
50-54	46,700	31,700
55-59	54,100	36,000
60-64	63,400	41,300
65 plus	70,200	45,100

TABLE D—PARENT CONTRIBUTION

Adjusted Available Income (AAI)	Parent Contribution
To minus $3,409	-$750 (negative figure)
Minus $3,409 to plus $10,000	22% of AAI
$10,001 to $12,500	$2,200 plus 25% of AAI over $10,000
$12,501 to $15,100	$2,825 plus 29% of AAI over $12,500
$15,101 to $17,600	$3,579 plus 34% of AAI over $15,100
$17,601 to $20,100	$4,429 plus 40% of AAI over $17,600
$20,101 or more	$5,429 plus 47% of AAI over $20,100

TABLE E—ASSET PROTECTION ALLOWANCE, INDEPENDENT STUDENT

Age	Single	Married
25 & Under	$ 0	$ 0
26	1,600	2,300
29	6,500	9,100
32	11,300	16,000
35	16,200	22,900
38	21,100	29,700
40	24,300	34,300
50	30,200	44,100
65	45,100	70,200